Sitting at His feet

Developing ears to hear the voice of Jesus

ADAM LIVECCHI

Sitting at His Feet

Developing Ears to Hear the Voice of Jesus

Adam LiVecchi

All Scripture taken from the King James Version which is in the Public Domain.

SITTING AT HIS FEET

ISBN 978-0-9835523-7-6

©2012 by Adam LiVecchi. All rights reserved. This book is protected by the copyright laws of the United States of America. No part of this publication may be reproduced, stored in a retrieval system, or transmitted in any form or by any means electronic, mechanical, photocopying, recording, or otherwise, without the prior written permission of the publisher or under consentual agreement.

Printed in the United States of America.

First Printing: February 2012

Cover art done by Ryan Smyth, Royal Essex. www.RoyalEssex.com

For more information on how to order this book or any of the other materials We See Jesus Ministries offers please contact:

We See Jesus Ministries
www.WeSeeJesusMinistries.com

Dedication

I dedicate this book to the only true and living God who is alive and who speaks. My desire is that everyone who reads this book will be drawn to the feet of Jesus to develop ears that hear, eyes that see, feet that go and hands that reach. Jesus, you are still my very best friend!

I would also like to dedicate this book to my brother, Aaron LiVecchi. Your relentless pursuit of Jesus when no one is looking shows the true strength of your heart. I am very proud of you!

Special Thanks & Acknowledgments

I want to acknowledge my beautiful wife **Sarah** for all she is in my life. She always encourages me; I don't remember her ever saying one discouraging word to me. Sarah, you are a crown to my head.

I would also like to acknowledge and honor my **Father and Mother, Angelo and Andrea LiVecchi** for being so supportive and helpful in every way. I want to thank my brother **Aaron** for being so faithful to Jesus. I am so proud of you for allowing God to separate you unto himself for his purposes.

I would also like to acknowledge **Steve and Christina Stewart** for being amazing spiritual parents. I would also like to acknowledge **John and Nancy Natale** for always being there for me even in the hard times. I am also very grateful to **Abner Suarez** for being a great friend.

A special thank you to the We See Jesus Ministries Board members: **Abner Suarez, John Natale, and Mac Barnes**.

I would also like to thank my friend **Ryan Smyth** for his graphic art work.

I would also like to thank **Julia Hali** for her help with editing.

Endorsements

As I read *Sitting at His Feet*, most of it in a single sitting. Page after page, I was challenged and encouraged by Adam's insights. He confronts us with both the cost and power of a life committed to hearing and obeying the One who loves us. I have traveled with Adam LiVecchi on many occasions to the developing world. This has given me the unique opportunity to observe first-hand his lifestyle of faith and obedience, as well as his great passion for Jesus and compassion for people. This book is not theory but the fruit of a life that is being lived well.

Steve Stewart
Founder of Impact Nations
Author of *When Everything Changes*
www.ImpactNations.com

Throughout the years as a friend and ministry partner to Adam, I have seen a voice that has come forth from the depths of Jesus. It has been an incredible journey for him and he has been faithful to the calling on his life. He has demonstrated to the body of Christ and me that he is passionate for the things that Jesus has called him to do and say. His character and integrity outweighs his anointing and his ability to write what he hears Jesus saying is unique. I know you will agree with me that his writings are a true inspiration to the people of God and also bring revelation to the hungry.

John Natale
Founder of John Natale Ministries
Co-Founder of Voices in the Wilderness School of the Prophets and Co-Author of *Listen.Learn.Obey.*
www.JohnNatale.net
www.VoicesintheWilderness.us

Adam LiVecchi consistently amazes me and everyone else that he ministers to. God has a great champion in Adam LiVecchi, and He continually gives Adam something new, something revelatory, and something useful to say. It is not only Adam's consistent work as a minister of God, but also God's work in Adam that makes reading his books a pleasure.

Rev, Mac Barnes
Founder of HaitiCharity.org - a ministry that feeds the poor and preaches the gospel in Haiti, also Author of *Total Wealth*.
www.HaitiCharity.org
www.PreciousPearl.us

Adam LiVecchi's "*Sitting at His Feet*" is a clear call from heaven for the body of Christ to become a generation of burning and shining lamps. This book is a map that will help to enable the body of Christ become a people who not only hear clearly what the Father is saying but who also declare what He is saying with great boldness. In this hour of great transition in the body of Christ, Adam's book clearly articulates what the Spirit is saying to the Church's and the hindrances to hearing what He is saying. Be stirred, impacted and changed forever by this powerful book.

Abner Suarez
Founder of For such a time as this, Inc
www.AbnerSuarez.com

Foreword

Adam LiVecchi is passionate about Jesus. I say that every time I hang up the phone with him. There is nothing that stands out as strong as his intense burning desire to see Jesus glorified. I am always refreshed and refocused by spending time listening to him revealate about the Lord. I am excited to be able to stand behind him as his passionate voice is spread far and wide through a new medium, the written word. If Adam is speaking, I am listening, and I recommend that others do the same. Adam's heart desires to see the Body of Christ rise up into the Glorious Bride without spot or wrinkle. Writing from this angle, he takes aim at the heart of the reader and attacks much of what I call *"Churchianity."* It is time to put on the apron, get out the steak sauce and head to the backyard BBQ because there is nothing that Adam likes more than *"Sacred Cows."*

Jonathan Welton
Founder of Jonathan Welton Ministries and Author of School of the Seers and Normal Christianity.
www.JonWelton.com

Table of Contents

Introduction 15
The Audible Voice of God and
Jesus Speaking from the Least of These

Chapter 1 21
Since the Beginning

Chapter 2 25
Come Out of Hell

Chapter 3 31
What is God's Voice Like?

Chapter 4 39
From the Garden to the Wilderness

Chapter 5 47
From the Wilderness to the Voice in the Wilderness

Chapter 6 55
The Audible Voice of God in the Life of Jesus

Chapter 7 65
The Posture of Humility

Chapter 8 73
Creating a Sustainable Atmosphere Where God Can Speak

Chapter 9 83
The Mind of Christ

Chapter 10 93
A Godly Life and Spiritual Sight

Chapter 11 103
Hearing Discipline

Chapter 12 113
Hearing Hindrances

Chapter 13 127
There is a Sword in His Mouth

Chapter 14 141
Maturing in Our Ability to Hear the Voice of God

Chapter 15 153
God is Speaking

Chapter 16 165
God Speaks Many Languages

Final Thoughts 175
The Urgency of His Voice

Introduction

The audible voice of God and Jesus speaking from the least of these

I would like to begin this book by thanking the Father for giving Jesus and thanking Jesus for sending the Holy Spirit to us. I will share some encounters that I have had with God's voice that changed my life forever. One of these five encounters was the Audible voice of God. It was a beautiful fall day on *October 21, 2007*. I was attending a wedding of a friend of mine in **New Jersey**. I was happy that my friend was getting married, but the atmosphere seemed more like a nightclub than a Christian marriage celebration. My car was parked all the way in the back of the parking lot. So I left the wedding to move my car. I really wanted to leave but for some reason I just could not. In a few minutes I was going to find out exactly why. While I was outside in my car, I was telling the Lord how much I hate lukewarm Christianity and asking him why do we Christians mistreat Jesus so much? I was in tears. God was breaking my heart and opening my eyes. He was showing me that often the church, including myself, is no different from the world. So after a few moments, I went back inside to see a whole bunch of Christians outside tipsy on booze and smoking cigarettes. That's just what I wanted to see—more Christians acting just like the world.

When I went back in, I sat back down at my table. No one was there; they were either smoking or dancing. As I was sitting there, I heard, "*Adam.*" I looked around and no one was anywhere near me. At that moment my mind told me something supernatural was happening. A few seconds later again I heard, "*Adam.*" The second time was a lot louder and a lot clearer. This voice came over me like a warm blanket. I could not move for at least a minute or two. This voice literally scared the hell out of me. I knew this was the God who spoke the world into existence. This was the voice that caused the earth to shake. After I gained my composure and was able to move again I got up and drove home silently. I even wore my seat belt, which was rare at the time. This shook me from the inside out. As I was driving home, the thoughts kept coming to me, *"What do you want from me, Lord?"* This encounter with God's audible voice caused me to search the scriptures and study the people who God called their name twice. This was a fascinating study. Before I did that study, I knew I had a calling to preach and demonstrate the gospel, but that study made me understand the seriousness of God's calling on my life. I still felt like that encounter had a more specific meaning. It was at a wedding; what did that mean? Anyway, I did not have any real answers until after I preached in a small church in Passaic, New Jersey.

December 9th, 2007. After I preached at a small Macedonian church the Pastor, Pastor Zoran pulled me aside and asked if he could pray for me. So I said sure, go ahead. He began to prophesy over me and say, *"The Lord knows you by name. He loves you with an everlasting love. He has hidden you, but soon he will release you."* Then he said, *"TV and radio."* As soon as he said, *"The Lord knows you by name,"* I was on the floor quicker than you can blink, in a puddle of tears. Immediately, I knew that the audible voice encounter I had at the wedding several months earlier was Jesus answering my prayers to want to know him. Now God was saying to me, I have heard your cry to want to know me, and I know you also. This messed me up forever because my life long goal is to really know Jesus. I want to be as close to Jesus at the marriage supper of the Lamb as John the beloved and Daniel the beloved. My ambition is to know God. That is the pursuit of my heart when no one is looking; he is what I am after. This book is written so that ears are opened to hear and that eyes are opened to see the beauty of God's only begotten Son Jesus. Our purity is his number one priority, and the word that he speaks to us makes us clean. We are his bride and we must be spotless. His voice is to cleanse us and lead us.

As I began to follow God's call on my life, it took me all over the world. He put a love in my heart for the poor. *February 2008* while I was with Impact Nations in **India** God spoke to me in a profound way. I was at a medical clinic in south India. It was hot, humid and pouring rain. I was standing in line with an elderly man. I was being friendly with him so I gave him a hug as an action of love because I could not speak his language. When I hugged him, immediately Jesus spoke to me. He said, *"I was sick and you came to me."* When I heard this, I began to weep like a baby. Jesus had just spoken to me from the least of these. He said whatever you do unto the least of these you do to me, and so he spoke from the person he identifies himself with in Matthew 25:35-36 which says, *"For I was hungered, and ye gave me meat: I was thirsty, and ye gave me drink: I was a stranger, and ye took me in: Naked, and ye clothed me: I was sick, and ye visited me: I was in prison, and ye came unto me."* I knew this was Jesus speaking to me because he said, *"I was sick and you came to me."* This rocked my world. After that I lost ability to function for a while, this had such a traumatic effect on my soul. For the rest of the day I worked in the medical clinic totally messed up and full of joy unspeakable.

As the journey continued in *September of 2009*, I was in **Montevideo, Uruguay**. In the beginning of the trip, my friend Teofilo Hayashi and I prayed for a woman with a tumor, and it instantly disappeared. Later on this same trip, we were walking to church on Sunday morning. I saw a street boy who looked hungry so I invited him in to have coffee and breakfast with me. It was he and I sitting at the table. As he was sitting there with me eating, I was telling him that Jesus loved him in Spanish. I stopped and said to the Lord, *"He really smells, Lord."* Immediately Jesus responded to me, *"What, Adam, you do not like the way I smell? I was hungry and you gave me food."* Here again Jesus was speaking in the face of the least of these. As I was sitting with this young man who is way too young to be homeless, I was weeping because of what Jesus just said. This really blew me away. I felt like I got saved all over again when the Lord spoke to me about the boy's smell. The boy then comes with us to church and sits in the front row with my friend Teofilo and I.

Later in the service he gets saved. As I sat by the homeless, I learned more about the fragrance of Christ than in any church service. This experience had a profound effect on my heart because I cannot forget the stench of that boy, which was really the fragrance of Christ in the face of the least of these.

About a month later, in **New Jersey** in *October of 2009* I hosted my first Prophetic Conference called *"Awake to Righteousness."* I had some food prepared in the back for the speakers. When service was over and the speakers and I went back to eat some amazing Cuban sandwiches. I noticed there were several people back there that were not invited. Usually I have no problem being strong with people but that time I did not for some reason. Several "down and outers" were back there eating with the speakers and I. So later that night I said, *"Lord do these people just not respect my authority because I am young or something? Is that why they were back there?"* Jesus said, *"No you prayed to be like me and these are the kind of people I attract."* Well out come the tears and confession and repentance all over again. Now Jesus is speaking on behalf of the down and outers. Religious hierarchies and boundaries mean nothing to King Jesus. Quite frankly, he would probably rather eat with the "down and outers" than the conference speakers or Bishop so and so. We must learn to calibrate our hearts to hear what Jesus is saying even if it goes beyond our religious thinking of how something should be.

Carrefour Haiti, *January 12, 2010*. This earthquake shook Haiti and brought a nation to its knees in thirty seconds. I happened to be there during the quake. I was in the epicenter of the quake and God miraculously spared my life. I was able to come out and return in February of 2010 and then three other times that year. The Lord allowed me to experience what he said in his word. *"Whose voice then shook the earth: but now he hath promised, saying, Yet once more I shake not the earth only, but also heaven."* (Hebrews 12:26) I love this scripture; it has become flesh in me because I lived through this experience of God's voice. That same voice that called my name twice and scared the hell out of me literally shook the earth.

When I came back from Haiti that February, I stayed in **Bavaro, Dominican Republic** for a few days to relax and also preach. One day I was walking back from the Internet café. As I was walking back to the church, I saw a Haitian in the garbage eating. So I grunted at him and signaled for him to get out of the trash and so he did. I walked over to him and gave him enough money for a decent meal because he was obviously hungry. His shirt was shredded, so I took my tank top off and gave it to him. As I walked away discouraged about this poor man's condition, I took my golf shirt out of my book bag and put it on. Then suddenly the Lord spoke to me and said, *"That is how you feel about me, you gave me the cheaper shirt and you kept the nice one for yourself."* So I asked Jesus to forgive me for giving him the cheaper shirt. Jesus needed to be clothed in the face of the needy, but I was more concerned about me. When Jesus speaks to you, it will cause you to see yourself, people and life for what it really is. This messed me up and showed me I am messed up. I was honored that he would even say something like this to me. He trusted that I would know it was him, and not try to bind the devil when it was actually Jesus speaking. The sharpness of Jesus' word cut into my heart and made me aware of its hardness. Then he was able to come in and touch it and heal it and make it tender to his voice. A heart that is tender to his voice will be generous toward others, even at the expense of self. It is a good thing when the Lord brings correction into our life. It may not feel good but the long-term results are worth a little temporary pain, and besides Jesus gave us the comforter to help us through the rough times.

Carrefour Haiti on *August 8, 2010*. It was a humid night, and I was doing an open-air crusade in not the nicest of neighborhoods. There were roughly 1500 people there. It began to pour and pour as I was preaching so I got off the stage and told the people that since they were wet I was going to get wet and pray for anyone and everyone who needed prayer. So a huge crowd of people came forward for prayer. So the prayer team went down to pray for the sick and demonized. People were getting healed and demons were being cast out. One thousand people stayed in the rain to dance and praise Jesus; it was beyond words. I had joy unspeakable. After I had finished praying for the people who were in line, I began to dance and sing and scream Jesus. Then a few moments later I stopped and looked into the crowd. When I focused on the crowd, I began to choke up and tear. It was then when Jesus spoke to me and said, *"This is why I said blessed are the poor for theirs is the kingdom."* I fell apart and started crying and dancing and thanking Jesus for speaking and allowing me to be around people who love him so very much. Please remember to listen for Jesus because you never know when he will say something that will change your life forever. I hope you are blessed richly in Christ as you continue to read this book.

Chapter 1
Since the Beginning

Since the beginning of time, up until now, there has been a simple problem. The problem is that people have a hard time hearing God for themselves. Hearing God for other people is often easier than hearing God for ourselves. Many people can tell others what they should do but have a hard time knowing what they themselves should do. This spiritual immaturity must be dealt with once and for all. The gift of prophecy is not a substitute for an authentic relationship with Jesus. Now is the time, this is the book, and we are the people. God is committed to our process of maturing; he desires that we grow up unto the measure of the fullness of his Son. Meaning he wants us to be like Jesus. This happens as Christ is formed in us. *Christ is formed in us as God speaks to us.* Our relationship with God is defined by his commitment to us and by his desire to communicate with us, simply because he loves us. If our commitment and communication with God are firm and clear, we will be full of everything God truly has for us in this life and in the age to come.

Isaiah 64:4 says, *"For since the beginning of the world men have not heard, nor perceived by the ear, neither hath eye seen, O God, beside thee, what he hath prepared for him that waiteth for him."* When it says *"O God, beside thee,"* Isaiah the Prophet is referring to Jesus. Jesus knew exactly what the Father had for him. That is why you hear Jesus say, *"For this purpose have I come, the hour is come that the Son of Man should be glorified, save me from this hour: but for this cause came I unto this hour."* Jesus knew what he came for and he knew when it was going to be made manifest. This information came by him hearing his Father. God wants our ears to hear and our eyes to see what he has for us, because Jesus did, and he is our example in all things.

If Adam and Eve truly knew what God had prepared for them, perhaps they would not have eaten the fruit from the tree of the knowledge of good and evil. Many people live miserable Christian lives by still eating from that tree daily. Many preachers get their sermons from that tree. The Father desires that we eat from the Tree of Life instead. The way we eat from the Tree of Life is by hearing what God is saying. His words are spirit and life; therefore, to eat we must hear. Hearing would be eating and fruit bearing would be obeying. The Tree of the knowledge of good and evil deals with facts and rules, while the Tree of Life deals with truth, life and experiences what God has said and promised. We have to choose what we want. The people who eat from the Tree of the knowledge of good and evil are those who have a hard time hearing God's voice. When Adam and Eve had eaten the forbidden fruit of that tree, they began to hide from the Presence of the Lord that was manifested or released when he spoke to them. When God speaks, his presence is released. *As God speaks to us, his voice is meant to bring us closer to him and make us more like him.* His voice is simply supposed to draw us to him because he loves us. God loves and knows therefore he speaks so that we can experience his love and know what he desires us to know him.

When we begin to hear God clearly, everything about us begins to change. Most people who do not hear God are fearful, disappointed and frustrated. According to the scriptures, that is the complete opposite of what a Christian should be like. We should be full of love, which leaves no room for fear; we should be full of hope and faith. *As we learn to listen to God and hear him we will truly become Christ-like.* There is no greater joy than to know God. The primary way we get to know God in this life is by him speaking and us listening. This happens when we are walking through life or reading the Bible. It happens at work or at church. We hear God when we give him our attention. If we are going to proceed in life and have good success, we must hear the proceeding word that is coming from God's mouth. Understanding the necessity of hearing God's voice will give birth to wisdom; wisdom is received as we hear God speak.

> *"The fear of the Lord is the beginning of wisdom: and the knowledge of the holy is understanding."* (Proverbs 9:10)

Wisdom is one of God's attributes. This attribute is supposed to navigate the decisions we make. The fear of the Lord is the beginning of wisdom; wisdom can be seen in our actions. Wisdom can be heard in our words, but ultimately it comes from God's mouth.

> *"For the Lord giveth wisdom: out of his mouth come knowledge and understanding."* (Proverbs 2:6)

One of the ways the Lord gives is by speaking. The way the enemy steals, is by stealing what God has said or by distracting us from what he is saying. This was how the enemy was successful with Adam and Eve. *If we do not remember what God has said, it becomes easy for the enemy to steal from us.* However, the enemy cannot have success with you or me if we hear God and obey consistently. I truly believe that you desire this above all things. This book is to assist you in your ability to recognize what God has said, is saying and what he will say. I say that you do have ears to hear what the Spirit of the Lord is saying to the church, and I believe that you have courage to obey God. God really believes in us and trusts us therefore we should start believing and trusting one another. When Jesus said in Revelation, *"He that hath an ear to hear, let him hear what the Spirit saith unto the churches."* He actually believed that people would hear and obey. That is why he spoke with the expectation that people will hear and obey. He expects us to hear and obey which releases faith in us to behave like the new creations he created us to be in him.

Questions

Wait quietly with a journal and write down what he says. By valuing what he says it will show him you really believe he is worth listening to. Jesus is an Author and he really likes when you write down what he says to you.

1. Ask God what he has for you to do to express who Jesus really is to those who need him most around you?

2. Are you eating from the knowledge of the tree of good and evil or are you eating from the tree of life?

Prayer

Father, I thank you that you have given me ears to hear. I pray that the Spirit of Wisdom and Revelation would come upon me as I read this book. Show me how to get life directly from you, Jesus.

Chapter 2
Come Out of Hell

God is good; therefore, he is in a good mood. God is so good he gives us choices; he is so smart he knows what decisions we will make even before we make them. He gives blessing for obedience and cursing is a direct result of disobedience. Any area of disobedience in our lives will be evident by the curse of sin and death that is in operation. Sin leads to death and death leads to hell. Many people are afraid to say that, but it is just as true now as when it was written in the Bible over 2,000 years ago. *Christians can live in hell on the inside and do all the right things on the outside.* Hundreds of thousands of Christians live like this today. They do good things but feel bad. The issue is that they struggle hearing God's voice; however, they are only one prayer away from the abundant life Christ promised. *Abundant life is not measured in dollars and cents but in us hearing God and obeying him.* As we hear God and obey him he manifests himself to us, which would be a great definition of Biblical Christianity. The only kind of Christianity is Biblical Christianity.

There was a time when God was silent to King David and he cried out to God and God heard him. God responded to him, which gave him experience. He penned those experiences down for us. We are invited into an experience with God, through David's testimony. To know about David's testimony with God simply is not enough. We need to experience the God of David and not just merely read what David said about God. For too long we have been satisfied with crumbs from the master's table, when there has been a feast prepared for us. Let us feast on Jesus as we hear his voice and obey his word. *"Jesus saith unto them, My meat is to do the will of him that sent me, and to finish his work."* (John 4:34)

Often when Christians come from a good church service you might hear them say, "That word was good; I was really fed spiritually." The truth is we aren't fed until we do what we have heard. Jesus said *"my food is to do the will of him who sent me."* We need to be like Moses and know God's ways. Israel knew what God did but they didn't know him. Moses partnered with God and he knew God. As we get to know God we see his works and learn his ways. However, it is not only about his works or his ways, but it becomes more and more about him as we mature. Maturity looks like us being conformed into his image by his word through his Spirit as we hear his voice. David had all that God could give, but what David really wanted was God. The question is what do we want? I believe God's voice and presence is the deepest cry of every person created in his image and likeness.

Listen to the cry of David's heart; it very may be the cry of your heart also. Psalm 28: 1 says, *"Unto thee will I cry, O Lord my rock, be not silent to me: lest if thou be silent to me, I become like them that go down into the pit."* **Hell on earth is not hearing God's voice.** God designed us to have a desire that can only be satisfied by him speaking to us personally. Our intimacy with Jesus grows as he speaks to us and his word takes root in us. As his word takes root in us, he is formed in us and we become like him. Becoming like Jesus is expressed through Character and Power, not one or the other but both. The word that takes root is the word that bears fruit. The more intimate we are with Jesus the more we will be like him. When we are really like him we can represent him properly to those who do not know him. We will be surprised to see how many people want him when they see what he is really like.

When David was crying out for God to speak in Psalm 28, he was actually crying out for God himself. David was longing for God's voice because he is the Word and when his voice is heard his word is imparted. He is his Word, hence John 1:1 which says, *"In the beginning was the Word, and the Word was with God, and the Word was God."* As God's voice is heard his Word then comes to live in us. The word that is in us makes us like him and keeps us from sinning.

> *"Thy word have I hid in mine heart that I might not sin against thee."* (Psalm 119:11)

Not sinning is simply not enough although it is a great start; however, we must know and experience him. The knowledge of God is released as he communicates with us. Christianity has been limited to a whole lot of "can't do's" for way too long, but the truth is there are a lot of "can do's." This is why Paul said, *"I can do all things through Christ who strengthens me."* I am merely echoing Paul's encouragement to the Philippians. So what you can do is hear God because Jesus said, *"My sheep hear my voice."* You can hear Jesus speak because you are his sheep. You can hear the Father speak because you are his child. You can hear the Holy Spirit speak because he is living inside of you. Perhaps at the end of this book you will not only be able to discern and know God's voice, but you will also know who or which person of the God-head is speaking to you. As we mature in our hearing and our study of the scriptures, we will know if the Father, Son or Holy Spirit is speaking.

The awesome thing about the God we serve is that he is the only true and living God. There is no other name under heaven in which men might be saved. (Referring to the name of Jesus Christ.) So that means because he is alive he speaks to us, initiating conversations at times and at other times he responds to us. Ask a Muslim or a Hindu or a Catholic who prays to saints, when the last time their God spoke to them and see their jaw drop and say, "I don't ever remember my God speaking to me." Then you can tell them that Jesus Christ who is risen from the dead loves them enough to speak to them. If they don't believe you, dare them to ask him to speak to them with a sincere heart of faith. A God who is alive and speaks is truly joy unspeakable. It is beyond words; it is something you must taste and see for yourself. Sometimes before we see, we must taste. *Meaning, an experience with God gives us spiritual sight of what he is really like.* Take note that this happened in the life of David. *However, the Holy Scriptures must be used to measure the integrity of these experiences.* The only scriptures that are Holy are written in the sixty-six books of the Bible. *The scriptures are not given because we do not need an encounter with God.* The scriptures are given to bring us into an encounter with the Word himself. There are times where experience is necessary before something can be properly described or understood. That is why sometimes you will hear this expression, "You had to be there." It is really rough for someone who is trying to describe something indescribable especially if they have not experienced what they are trying to describe. In Psalm 28, David was crying out to God because he was desperate for the voice of God. Evidently God responded to him because Psalm 29 specifically focuses on describing the voice of the Lord and the effects of his voice. The God of the Bible is alive; therefore, he responds to the cries of his people. One of the main things that separate Christianity from ALL the other false religions is that our God is alive and he speaks.

As mentioned, David is crying out to God and praying for God to speak to him in Psalm 28. In the beginning of Psalm 29 he is worshipping then he begins to describe the voice of the Lord. Prayer and worship is the kind of atmosphere where we can experience the Lord's voice. If you have ever been in a church service and worship was cut short by Sister "the same prophecy every week," or Pastor "I need to be heard," you can feel an unexplainable disappointment. That is because the Lord desired to speak and people who wanted to speak on his behalf interrupted him because of their immaturity in his presence. This is only a sign of spiritual immaturity; it does not mean the people have a bad heart. It only means they do not have a fined tuned ear. Prayer and worship create an atmosphere that is conducive to God speaking. Many people do not hear from God simply because they do not speak to him or if they do they do not expect him to speak back, which causes them to end prayer when they run out of requests. If David had ended his prayer and worship time when he was done, he would not have been able to write Psalm 29, which describes what the voice of the Lord is like. Sometimes we have to get to the end of ourselves so we can hear God and experience his voice and presence.

Here is one of David's conclusions on God's voice. Psalm 29:4 states, *"The voice of the Lord is powerful; the voice of the Lord is full of majesty."* The word powerful in this verse means ability, strength, might, force, and substance. All of those words are victorious words that effect change both in and around us. The word majesty in this verse means magnificence, beauty, honor, glory, splendor and comeliness. The Lord Jesus uses the beauty of his voice to draw us to him. *God's presence is directly attached to his voice; they are inseparable.* We will look back at Psalm 28 and look forward to Psalm 143 to tie God's voice and his presence together. Psalm 28: 1 says, *"Unto thee will I cry, O Lord my rock, be not silent to me: lest if thou be silent to me, I become like them that go down into the pit."* Psalm 143:7-8 states, *"Hear me speedily, O Lord: my spirit faileth: hide not thy face from me, lest I be like unto them that go down into the pit. Cause me to hear thy loving-kindness in the mourning; for in thee do I trust: cause me to know the way wherein I should walk; for I lift up my soul unto thee."* **Hell on earth is living on earth with the absence of God's voice and presence.** David again is crying out to God for his face or presence He is also crying out for direction in his life as well as God's voice of loving-kindness. Everyone truly wants God's presence and his voice. The scriptures say, *"No good thing will he withhold from them who walk uprightly."* When God is withholding something from us, it's usually because we are withholding ourselves from him. God's voice and his presence is our portion because we are his inheritance. We are his purchased possession. Therefore, he wants to speak to us and through us. The beauty of his voice will draw us into the beauty of his holiness. This will continually happen until his beauty rests on us and he establishes the work of our hands by telling us "the way you should walk." David said, *"For I lift my soul unto thee."* When you put your mind will and emotions in God's hands, it is impossible not to hear his voice.

Questions

1. Is there any open disobedience to God in your life, which has been a roadblock for you? If so confess and ask God for the strength to walk in obedience.

2. Do you need to ask God or a Pastor or leader who you feel has hindered you from God's presence in a church service by interrupting worship to forgive you? Perhaps you should ask God to forgive you for judging someone because of his or her spiritual immaturity in discerning God's presence.

Prayer

Father, forgive me for judging someone's heart based on my spiritual immaturity. Lord Jesus help me to live in your presence. Let the beauty that comes from your voice rest upon my life and draw people to you. Establish the work of my hands so I can be a blessing to others in Jesus' name.

Chapter 3
What is God's Voice Like?

God's voice is simply supernatural. God is naturally supernatural. When we hear and obey God, we become naturally supernatural. I call that normal Christianity. This is what we were born for; we were born for his good pleasure.

"Now faith is the substance of things hoped for, the evidence of things not seen." (Hebrews 11:1)

So without faith it is impossible to please God. Paul said in Romans, *"Faith cometh by hearing and hearing the word of God."* So the beginning stages of pleasing God are to simply involve hearing him. The art of hearing is developed when we learn the discipline of listening. If we want to hear God speak, we must learn to be still and silent. What we set our affections on is what or whom we will listen to. We were created to please God and without hearing God we have no faith to please him. Therefore, our first priority must be to hear God. Faith is a substance. The word substance is also used when David described the voice of the Lord as powerful in Psalm 29:4. Powerful is also translated into the word substance. Faith gives us the power and ability to please the one who created us.

Since God's voice is powerful, it is also supernatural in nature. Whether we believe it or not, God commands us to do supernatural things. *When we obey his commands, we have access to his power.* His love for us causes him to command us to be supernatural; when we obey what he is saying, we become like the one who is speaking to us. It takes a renewed mind to truly believe what God says. Without a renewed mind we could not hear God even if He spoke to us audibly, see John 12:28-30. Often when God speaks, it is contrary to the natural realm or practical logic. We see this concept really clearly when God calls Moses to deliver Israel from Egypt.

In Exodus 3, God speaks to Moses out of a burning bush that is not consumed by fire. Let us analyze something for just a brief moment. Fire burns bushes to ashes and bushes do not talk. When Moses turned aside to see this phenomenon, God called his name twice, *"Moses, Moses."* After he called his name, he told him to take off his shoes because the place that he was standing was holy. God instructed him to have reverence when he approached him because wherever God is, is a Holy place. *When we approach God with reverence, we are positioning ourselves for revelation.* When we have reverence for his word, his voice will be heard. Then the Lord revealed himself to Moses. After the Lord revealed himself to Moses, he then revealed Moses' assignment to him. God imparts destiny through the knowledge of himself as he reveals himself.

In Moses' commissioning, he has two encounters with the voice of God and with his power that is accessed by obedience to what he is saying.

> Exodus 4:1-4 states, *"And Moses answered and said, But behold, they will not believe me, nor hearken unto my voice: for they will say, The Lord hath not appeared unto thee. And the Lord said unto him, what is in thine hand? And he said, A rod. And he said, Cast it on the ground, and it became a serpent; and Moses fled from before it. And the Lord said unto Moses, Put forth thine hand, and take it by the tail. And he put forth thine hand, and take it by the tail. And he put forth his hand, and caught it, and it became a rod in his hand."*

Moses was a shepherd; his rod was only operating in the natural to protect the sheep from wolves and whack the sheep if they got out of line. It served only a natural purpose. If you or I were to throw a rod on the grown, it would still be a rod, only it would now be a rod on the ground. However, when God told Moses to throw it on the ground, it became a serpent. I think God was clearly illustrating that he is the boss, that he is in charge and that his voice is powerful.

When Moses obeyed the voice of God, he had access to God's power. Then the Lord told him to pick the serpent up by its tail. Anyone in his or her right mind would not pick up a serpent by its tail. I am not a country boy and even I know if you pick up a snake by the tail, it will bite you. In order to pick up a snake you must pick it up very close to where the head and body meet so it cannot turn its face to bite you. Only someone with faith, only someone with a renewed mind, will pick up a snake by the tail. The carnal mind is enmity with God. One of the things that stops many people from being able to hear God is the carnal mind. *If our mind is at enmity with God, our ears will surely have a hard time hearing the person our mind is at war or in enmity with.* Moses grabbed the snake and it became a rod. Before God spoke to him and told him to grab it by the tail he was running from it. When God spoke to him, faith was released because faith comes by hearing the word of God. Faith gave him the courage to grab what he was previously running from. *Biblical faith gives us faith for the impossible.* The impossible is usually illogical. In order to love God with all of our mind, sometimes we have to turn it off and believe what he has said and simply obey him in spite of what we do or do not understand. If Moses' mind were in the natural world, he would not have grabbed that snake by the tail. The previous miracle of God speaking through a bush, that was not consumed, trained Moses' heart to believe God even though he knew he could not logically explain what he just saw. Based on what God had done and what he was saying, Moses had faith and courage to obey God. God did not bother to explain to Moses how he did it or even why. He was not interested in Moses understanding how he did it; he was only interested in Moses partnering with him in the deliverance of the Israelites. The cry of the people came before God and God and his voice came before Moses so he would be a deliverer in his generation. God's voice is coming to you so that you would be deliverer in this generation. The question is will you respond?

As Moses' encounter and commissioning continues, God's voice became more personal. This is what God desires for us— that his voice would become more personal. God's voice went from affecting the bush near Moses, to Moses' rod. God's government is increasing; the Lord is drawing near to Moses and it gets even better. Remember God's voice was speaking to Moses as part of his redemptive plan for his people Israel. God spoke to Moses to deliver his people because he made a promise to Abraham. So God spoke according to his redemptive plan. God's redemptive plan is important to understand as we mature in our ability to hear God's voice. A good majority of what God is saying is in context of the big picture, called his redemptive plan.

> "That they may believe that the Lord God of their father, the God of Abraham, the God of Isaac, and the God of Jacob, hath appeared unto thee. And the Lord said further more unto him, Put now thine hand into thy bosom. And he put his hand into his bosom: and when he took it out, behold, his hand was as leprous as snow. And he said, Put thine hand into thy bosom again. And he put his hand into his bosom again; and plucked it out of his bosom, and, behold, it was turned again as his other flesh." (Exodus 4:5-7)

So God affects the burning bush, which is close to him. Then he affects his rod, which belongs to him. Then he affects his hand, which is him. Here God's voice becomes more and more personal in the life of Moses. *The more personal God's voice is in our life the more we learn to trust him.* God was revealing his power to heal and his power to judge to Moses because he was about to judge Egypt and heal Israel. Moses' hand turning to leprosy was judgment and his hand turning back to normal was healing. Mercy really does triumph over judgment. God was in the process of making good on his promise to Abraham, Isaac and Jacob and Moses was going to be his instrument. The judgment of Egypt was part of God's redemptive plan for Israel. Similar to Jesus becoming sin so we could become the righteousness of God in him. God's judgment on his Son is what allows his redemption to purchase us. God's judgment on Egypt was his mercy on Israel.

When God speaks to us, he will tell us to do something that is not in our power to fully do without him. Many people only believe that God tells them to do things that they can do without him; however, Biblically speaking that is not true. Moses and Aaron could not deliver Israel without God. However, when they did what was in their power to do, God did what was in his power to do. They threw the rod down in front of Pharaoh and his magicians and Moses' and Aaron's rod swallowed all the magicians' rods. That was God who did that, but their job was to throw it down in the obedience of faith. As they did what they could do, God did what he could do.

We can only co-labor with Christ when we hear his voice and obey his word. The Spirit of God begins to move in our life when we obey God's word. This will put a smile on the Father's face. This is what we were created for. This is why we are a new creation in Christ Jesus created for good works. We were created for good works and not merely comfortable pews. It is in our "DNA" to hear God and obey him. I have even heard Christians, or unbelieving believers, quote Jeremiah, *"The heart is deceitfully wicked who can know it?"* What I say to that is those were unbelievers, and Jesus has promised us in the book of Ezekiel a new heart, a heart of flesh. *That heart is tender towards God's word and receptive to God's voice.* Jesus' heart was ruptured and broken so we could have a new one. God is not stupid; he does not give us a deceitfully wicked heart and then tell us he is taking us on the journey of all Truth as the Spirit speaks and leads. Hearing God's voice through the scriptures, through dreams and visions and through accountable and integral prophetic ministry is what will allow us to see God and experience him for what he is really like. Jesus Christ is God and he showed us what the Father is really like. Jesus said, *"If you have seen me you have seen the Father."* He is the Word made flesh, yet he did not speak his own words. He only spoke what he heard from his Father. Jesus' main priority was to hear the Father, yet he himself was God. He was, is and always will be the Word, yet he did not speak his own words. That is a perfect picture of self-control. How much more should we understand our need to hear God for ourselves? We are not the Word, and we certainly are not God, or even little gods as false teachers teach. We are his people created in his image and likeness, who were created to hear his voice. We were created to live in his presence and manifest his kingdom as we obey his word. It really is all about him.

Questions

1. Do you have a hard time hearing or believing that you have heard God?

2. Is it easier to believe God when he tells you something that is in your power to make happen versus something that you know only he can do?

Prayer

Father, please forgive my unbelief and help me believe what you are saying enough to obey you just as Jesus did.

Chapter 4
From the Garden to the Wilderness

God's redemptive plan has been made manifest through the ages by men and women who have heard his voice and obeyed him. Adam and Eve were seduced by the serpent to eat from the tree that God commanded them not to eat from and then they realized they were naked. *Our first and foremost covering is obedience to God's word. Spiritually, God covers us as we hear his voice and obey him. As great as my pastor and your pastor are, they cannot cover the shame of our nakedness when we disobey God's word.* When we obey God's word, we put on the Lord Jesus.

> *"But put ye on the Lord Jesus Christ, and make not provision for the flesh, to fulfill the lusts thereof."*
> (Romans 13:14)

The same way the Psalmist said, *"I have hid thy word in my heart that I might not sin against thee."* Here is the same concept: we put on Jesus by obeying his word, which makes sin no longer an option. To live we must hear because faith comes by hearing, and the just live by faith.

After Adam and Eve were clothed by Jesus and kicked out of the garden they repopulated the earth. Then it grew really evil, so God destroyed everyone by a flood. The only people who lived were the people who heard God's word. Noah built an ark and truly lived by what God was saying. After many years God spoke to Abram and told him to *"leave his father's house."* He left and then God, over a course of some time, made some amazing promises to him and changed his name to Abraham. If he had not obeyed God and left, he would not have been properly positioned for what God had for him. Abraham obeying what he did not understand is what prepared him for promises bigger than himself. *Obeying what we do not understand is God's way of preparing us for a blessing we cannot contain.* Abraham had a son, Isaac, according to God's promise. God asked Abraham to kill Isaac. So Abraham put Isaac on the altar and had the knife in the air ready to execute his son. The angel of the Lord spoke from heaven to Abraham and told him to stop. For a split second, Abraham felt the pain the Father would later feel as he would not stop the knife but pour out his wrath upon his very own Son Jesus. Isaac truly did live by every word that was proceeding from the mouth of God. *Our ability to hear from God directly affects whether other people live or die.* If Abraham had not heard God, his son would have been dead. In reality, God was not trying to kill Isaac; he was trying to kill Abraham. God was after the crucifixion of Abraham's flesh, not the death of Isaac. God wanted to see and even show Abraham that he loved him more than his promised son. We must love God more than what he gives us or what he can do for us.

Isaac lives because Abraham heard God and obeyed him. Isaac then has Jacob and Jacob has Joseph the dreamer. His favor causes his brothers to be jealous, so they sell him into slavery. *If people aren't jealous of us, we are not walking in real favor, remember real favor is not fair.* He did the right thing by not sleeping with Potiphar's wife and got the wrong results by being thrown in prison for his integrity. The word of the Lord tested him and he was found faithful. He later possessed the word of the Lord because he passed the test that the word of the Lord often brings with it. If we want to have the word of the Lord, it will test us first. If we desire the word of the Lord it must also have us. Joseph had a faithful heart and he emerged from the dungeon to the palace. *Faithfulness and perseverance will cause promotion in the kingdom.* In the palace the Pharaoh dreams a dream. Here we see God even speaks to sinners. God even speaks to people who do not read the Bible. The problem is that Pharaoh is not one of God's sheep and he does not hear his voice. Here is where Joseph the dreamer comes in. He hears God and interprets the dream. He saves the world by hearing God's voice and saving food for seven years. Joseph interprets someone's dream and his dream came true. *The way we get promoted into our destiny is by serving someone else in his or hers.* So the world did not starve because one man heard God and obeyed. Before Joseph died, he prophesied the freedom of his people.

The cry of Israel comes to the Lord and he sends Moses. Moses hears and obeys and God saves. After God had saved Israel with signs and wonders, he gave them a law. Before Moses could even give it to them they were already breaking it while God was writing it. Moses got mad at the people and threw the law down. In his anger he became just like the people he was angry at, a law breaker. Israel openly rejected God's voice because of fear. How many people reject the supernatural because of fear of deception? *Many believe the devil is better at deceiving them than God is at keeping that which belongs to him.*

> Exodus 20:18-20 states, *"And all the people saw the thunderings, and the lightnings, and the noise of the trumpet, and the mountain smoking: and when the people saw it they removed, and stood afar off. And they said unto Moses, Speak thou with us, and we will hear: but let not God speak with us, lest we die. And Moses said unto the people, Fear not: for God is come to prove you, and that his fear may be before your faces that ye sin not."*

Israel said no to God's voice and yes to Moses. They said no to God's voice and yes to his rules. This was to their own demise because it was the fear of him that was released from his voice that was able to keep them from breaking the rules. *Their encounter with God was to empower them to live according to God's law.* They responded in the natural to something supernatural and it only hurt them in the long run. Our natural tendencies are to fear what we do not understand. Sadly to say this usually winds up hurting us like it did Israel. *If you really have the peace of God ruling in you, then your peace will pass understanding.* If your peace does not pass your understanding, you need more peace. As Jesus slept in the storm his peace passed the disciples' understanding, and they thought he did not care about them. They thought he did not care if they all died.

The problem was they forgot that he had previously said to them, *"We are going to the other side."* When they did not remember what Jesus had said, their natural understanding outweighed their peace and they could not speak peace to a storm that they did not have peace in. Jesus said to the storm, *"Peace be still"* and peace was released because he had it to release. When we listen to God's voice and remember his word, we can have peace that passes understanding and we can speak to storms and circumstances and see them bow to name of Jesus.

When Moses began to relay God's commandments, statutes and judgments to the people, one of his first statements was *"Hear O Israel."* Before they were instructed to do anything, they were commanded to hear.

> *"Hear therefore, O Israel, and observe to do it; that it may be well with the, and that ye may increase mightily as the Lord God of thy Fathers hath promised thee, in the land that floweth with milk and honey. Hear, O Israel; The Lord our God is one Lord: And thou shalt love the Lord thy God with all thine heart, and with all thy soul, and with all thy might. And these words, which I command thee this day, shall be in thine heart."* (Deuteronomy 6:3-6)

When the scripture says, *"The Lord our God is one Lord,"* the word *one* literally means a man in Hebrew. This is speaking of Jesus the God man who will fulfill the law by loving God in perfect and complete obedience. This verse is revealing Jesus as fully God and fully man. Before God asks us to love him he reveals Jesus to us, so we can love God as Jesus did. Jesus is the standard. I am not the standard; your pastor is not the standard— Jesus is. We have the power to become sons because the Father gave his son. The first thing the Father wants us to hear is the revelation of who his Son is. Hearing is what empowers loving. Obedience to the word comes by hearing God's voice. What is very interesting is that the generation that said they did not want to hear God's voice did not inherit the

Promised Land. God's first priority is hearing. Hearing directly deals with the affections. The more we love someone the more we will listen to him or her.

Nations rise and fall by choosing to hear God and obey him or not to hear and not to obey. Israel did not only reject God's voice they rejected his leadership and wanted a King and so they got Saul, the people's choice. When God's voice is rejected, his leadership will also be rejected. His voice is his leadership. We can either have God's voice or the people's choice. Unfortunately, many people choose the people's choice. This is unfortunate because a direct result of rejecting God's voice and leadership is sickness and poverty and oppression. When Israel rejected God's voice, they also rejecting living in divine health. When they rejected his leadership, Saul taxed the life out of them. Jerusalem was besieged by Babylon because Israel's leadership rejected the scroll written by the Prophet Jeremiah; see Daniel 1 and Jeremiah 36. Cities are taken captive by the enemy when God's people do not live in subjection to his Word that is made manifest by his voice. God gave Moses and the people he took out of Israel a prophetic word. My paraphrase of this word is, "You guys are going to the promised land." Out of 3 million people only Joshua and Caleb made it in. Both Moses and the children of Israel did not go into what God had for them. The children of Israel rejected God's voice, which was what would have caused them to fear and obey him. They rejected his voice and did not fulfill the promise he had for them. *We live out the prophetic word over our life, by perpetually hearing his voice and obeying.* The word is fulfilled as his voice is heard and diligently observed. Moses did not openly reject God's voice; he disobeyed it. Disobedience is similar to rejection. The first time God brought water forth from a rock, he told Moses to hit the rock and out came the water. At the obedience of God's word, his power was made accessible.

The second time God told Moses to speak to the rock, but instead he hit the rock. By the grace of God, water came forth and the thirsty drank. However, this miracle was not God affirming Moses; it was merely God giving a drink to his people. God was not personally pleased with Moses, but he still used him in the supernatural. The power of God is not his affirmation of one's behavior or doctrine; it is simply God fulfilling his promise to someone else. Moses' direct disobedience cost him the Promised Land. He hit the rock because he was angry with the people because of their complaining. Moses killed an Egyptian in Egypt because he responded to injustice in the wrong spirit. Then he got angry with the people for breaking the law, and he threw it down and did the very thing he was mad at the people for—breaking the law. The last outburst of anger caused him to directly disobey God, which cost him God's best. God's love is for everyone; his best is for the obedient. Moses did not deal with his anger issue, and it finally dealt with him. When we allow the Lord to deal with our issues, our hearts become tender and our ears stay opened. When we lose the fear of the Lord, we lose our ability to hear the Lord and obey him. The fear of the Lord does not just cause us to hear the Lord; it causes us to obey him also. If we fear him, we will hear him. If we love him, we will obey him. When we obey him he manifests himself, and there is nothing greater than that. He is the Promised Land because all the promises of God are yes and amen in Christ Jesus.

Questions

1. Do you feel like you have walked in circles because you have not had clear direction from the Lord?

2. Is there some issue in your life that you haven't let the Lord deal with? Perhaps if there is, it's keeping you from experiencing God's promises for your life. Allow the Lord to deal with it before it deals with you.

Prayer

Father, I thank you for the freedom you gave me in your son Jesus. I thank you Father that the path of the just shines brighter and brighter unto the perfect day. I thank you that my path will become more apparent everyday in Jesus' name.

Chapter 5

From the Wilderness to the Voice in the Wilderness

Israel finally inherited the Promised Land. It took leaders with spiritual sight to get them there. They eventually went into captivity because they would not hear and obey God. *Captivity always follows disobedience.* Then God graciously released them from captivity in three waves. Eventually, God became silent. Before he became silent, he released a prophecy through the mouth of one of his friends.

> *"Behold, I will send you Elijah the prophet before the great and dreadful day of the Lord: And he shall turn the heart of the fathers to the children, and the heart of the children to their fathers, lest I come smite the earth with a curse."* (Malachi 4:5-6)

Historically, many people believe God was silent for about 400 years of human history. The question I have is, was God silent or were people just not listening? At this point it really does not matter because he is no longer silent in these last days, but he has spoken to us and is speaking to us by His Son Jesus.

If God was silent for those 400 years, he clearly breaks his silence continuing with the last topic he prophesied about before he became silent. God sent Gabriel the Angel who stands in the Presence of God to Zacharias the Priest. The Priest was talking to God and all of a sudden God sends the Angel Gabriel to talk to him. God seemed to continue right where he left off. In Malachi, God prophesied about a certain man then he stopped talking for 400 years. He continues, in the New Testament, with a conversation with the Father of the man he was talking about to his friend Malachi. From heaven's perspective, John the Baptist would be great.

> *"For he shall be great in the sight of the Lord, and shall neither drink neither wine nor strong drink; and he shall be filled with the Holy Ghost, even from his mother's womb. And many of the children of Israel shall he turn to the Lord their God. And he shall go before him in the Spirit and power of Elijah, to turn the hearts of the fathers to the children and the disobedient to the wisdom of the just; to make ready a people for the Lord."* (Luke 1:15- 17)

John was great in the sight of the Lord, which is one of the highest compliments in the entire Bible from God to man. *Sometimes greatness is not only defined by what you do, but also by what you do not do. Greatness is not only turning water into wine, but greatness is also not drinking any wine and being wholly separate from the world.* Greatness is simply defined by obedience. If we desire to be great in God's sight, we must simply hear his voice and obey his word. Hearing his voice and obeying his word will make us like him. When we are like him, we become naturally supernatural. Not only do we have Godly character, but we also have power to do what Jesus did.

There is a really simple, yet interesting principle that is visible to those who know the Lord's voice. God picked right back up where he left off. Often when God is trying to develop something to us that will mature us, we want to move on to something bigger or more exciting. If we are having trouble hearing God now, we must remember the last thing he said to us because that is what his wisdom chose to equip us with for this present moment. *When we remember what he said, we will begin to hear what he is saying. When we value what he has said, we position ourselves for what he is saying. True corporate unity comes when a group of people is willing to listen to God and obey him.* Everybody really wants to hear from the one who knows everything. His name is God, and he lives in you if you are born again. Even wicked people want to hear from God, which is why Pharaoh ended up speaking to Joseph. Also the King of Babylon sought out Daniel. Saul as a young man sought out Samuel. Saul was looking for a solution, so he went to a prophet not a psychic. *True prophetic ministry is a ministry of solutions, not merely Biblical problem analysis.* People are going to begin to search you out because you have ears to hear. To you it has been given to know the mysteries of the Kingdom, and people sure do have questions. When we have ears to hear we will be sought out because people really do want to hear from God. *There are psychics everywhere because people desire to hear from God, and the church has often been silent in society. We, as believers, owe the world an encounter with Jesus; however, we cannot give it to them if we do not hear him.* True ministry cannot be taught; it can only be received. Any ministry that is born of God's Spirit begins when God speaks or reveals something. If it comes from the flesh, it will only reap corruption. We have prophesied in church but have been silent in the city. If we desire to be a voice in the wilderness, we must leave the church building once and a while and speak God's point of view to a wicked and perverse generation. When we speak God's perspective, people receive an opportunity for repentance. *If we merely tell people repent and do not tell them how, we fail miserably to bring people to the real Jesus who has answers and solutions.*

John the Baptist emerged in a time of great darkness, yet he was a burning and shining lamp. The message he preached caused everyone who heard it to press into it. John was a Levite who never ministered in Jerusalem; he never even ministered in the temple. His place was the wilderness. The wilderness was about 18-20 miles outside of Jerusalem. Yet all of Jerusalem came to him to be baptized. God was silent for so long, people became so hungry that they would walk 18-20 miles to be baptized. There had to be supernatural strength on his voice because John the baptizer was not on the radio or the television, people were not seeing his website or YouTube channel. How did people know to wander at least 18-20 miles from Jerusalem to the wilderness, to be baptized? This was supernatural. John was preparing the way of the Lord; he was straightening the crooked paths. John was not afraid to call a spade a spade. He confronted both the religious and political system. He called the religious hierarchy of apostasy snakes and vipers. He even confronted Herod's adultery. This is just a little about John the baptizer. True prophetic voices are not afraid to confront the issues of their day. The same way that true warriors are not afraid to confront Goliath and his friends.

This voice in the wilderness was not afraid to confront the burning issues of the day. He did not sweep them under the rug in the name of *"edification and comfort."* There is too much tolerance in the church and too little revelation. Do not worry, this to is changing because God is speaking and we will be listening. The more we learn to listen to God the more we will be willing to obey. Learning to listen makes us willing to obey. When we obey, we can eat the fruit of obedience. When we tolerate things God does not, we lose reverence and trade it in for tolerance and relevance. *When we lose reverence, we lose revelation and the light in the house of God goes out like in the days of Eli the Priest.* This is how we know there is a leadership shift coming upon us swiftly. God is raising up voices in the wilderness to prepare the way of the Lord. If God were not speaking in the wilderness, then there would be no voice in the wilderness preaching. Our authority to speak comes from our privilege to hear.

> *"What I tell you in darkness, that speak ye in light: and what ye hear in the ear, that preach ye upon the housetops."*
> (Matthew 10:27)

The wilderness is the place where God changes the way we think. Our thinking is changed as his voice is heard. We are renewed in the Spirit of our mind as the Spirit of God speaks to us. John the baptizer preached, *"Repent the Kingdom of God is at hand."* He also said, *"Bring forth fruits worthy or repentance."*

> *"Bring forth therefore fruits worthy of repentance, and begin not to say within yourselves, We have Abraham to our father: for I say unto you that God is able of these stones to raise up children unto Abra-*

ham. And now also the axe is laid unto the root of the trees: every tree therefore which bringeth not forth good fruit is hewn down and cast into the fire. And the people asked him saying, What shall we do then? He answereth them, He that hath two coats, let him impart to him that hath none; and he that hath meat, let him do likewise. The came also the publicans to be baptized, and said unto him, Master, what shall we do? And he said unto them, Exact no more than that which is appointed you. And the soldiers likewise demanded of him, saying, And what shall we do? And he said unto them, Do violence to no man, neither accuse any falsely; and be content with you wages." (Luke 3:8-14)

In other words, show people that you have changed the way you think by changing the way you live. How someone thinks and lives is inseparable. John here was relevant but not tolerant. He addressed the issues of the day such as greed, extortion, false accusations and violence. What is interesting is he did not make a website about those people, but he addressed them personally. In our day we need to talk to people and not just talk about them. Watch what the next verse says. Luke 3:15 states, *"And as the people were in expectation, all men mused in their hearts of John, whether he was the Christ, or not."* Imagine if we heard and obeyed God's voice so much that people thought that we were Jesus. *Sadly to say people who do not really know Jesus have misrepresented him so much that many people do not even want to hear about him.* I have good news; you and I are going to be the people who are conformed to his image by hearing his voice. As this happens, we will represent him for who he really is. That is what the voices that God is raising up in this hour will do because the Spirit of Prophecy is the testimony of Jesus. The world needs to know God's heart and mind, but it will take our mouths to be opened for this to happen. Are you willing? Of course you are, Jesus died in faith that there would be a people who wholly live for him and his kingdom. Jesus believes in you.

God wants people who are outside the box, but inside the Word and led by his Spirit. John the Baptist was a Levite who never ministered in Jerusalem. John did not wear the Priestly garment; he wore animal skins, and he ate locusts. There was something radically different about him. He had God on the inside and did not care about the outside too much. He did not live in the house of God or minister there. He was the House of God filled with the Holy Spirit from his mother's womb, and he ministered from that place. John was a fiery preacher of righteousness, who declared God's word with no apologies. When we become relevant we really become irrelevant. When we try to "fit in" in order to bring change, the only thing that will change is us. We need to be wholly different. We are a peculiar people and we should stop apologizing for it.

> Matthew 3:11-13 says, *"I indeed baptize you with water unto repentance: but he that cometh after me is mightier than I, whose shoes I am not worthy to bear: he shall baptize you with the Holy Ghost, and with fire: Whose fan is in his hand, and he will thoroughly purge his floor, and gather his wheat into the garner; but he will burn up the chaff with unquenchable fire. The cometh Jesus from Galilee to Jordan unto John, to be baptized of him."*

So John the Baptist, a Levite, is in the wilderness preaching about judgment and the Savior shows up. Some would call him a *"judgment prophet."* However, Jesus still shows up when he speaks. Evidently the message of Judgment does not offend the Judge who came to seek and save that which is lost. Preaching should cause Jesus to show up. Preaching is not just for men and women to merely show off what they know. Preaching should bring about the movement of the Spirit; it should cause God's presence and power to be manifested. It is more about whom we know, than what we know. John's message and ministry was consummated suddenly when Jesus showed up on the scene as he was preaching. Jesus is the main event. All true prophetic ministry points to and reveals Jesus.

Questions

1. Are you an analysis expert or are you giving people solutions for their life through the wisdom of God, who is Christ Jesus?

2. Are you willing to speak the truth in love even if it costs you relationships that you value?

Prayer

Father, I ask you to give me courage to speak the truth in love. Lord, I ask that I would love you enough to speak your perspective into the people and circumstances that surround my life, in Jesus' name I pray.

Chapter 6

The Audible Voice of God in the Life of Jesus

So as John the baptizer is preaching in the wilderness, Jesus the Lamb of God comes onto the scene. This is what he says to John in Matthew 3:15, *"And Jesus answering him said unto him, Suffer it to be so now: for thus it becometh us to fulfill all righteousness. Then he suffered him."* John was to baptize Jesus to fulfill the law because it was the Levite's duty to consecrate the Lamb for Passover. Therefore, John the Levite consecrated Jesus, the Lamb for Passover. It was not done in the temple; it was outside the box but inside the Word. As the Levites were bearing the Ark of the Covenant on their shoulders, the waters of the Jordan River split. When this Levite baptized the Lamb of God consecrating him for Passover, the heavens split open. The same river, before the rivers split, now the heavens split. The heavens split so God can speak and be heard by those who are listening. The heavens are opened beloved now we must open our ears and pay attention to the Lord.

Let us hear what God was saying as heaven was opened, Matthew 3:16-17 says, *"And Jesus, when he was baptized, went up straightway out of the water: and, lo, the heavens were opened unto him, and he saw the Spirit of God descending like a dove, and lighting upon him, And lo a voice from heaven saying, This is my beloved Son, in whom I am well pleased."* The Father is affirming his Son. The Father is declaring that this is the Lamb that will take away the sins of the world. He is affirming his Son as a blameless and spotless Lamb who is consecrated to be slain. Here we see a family reunion. The Father is speaking from heaven; the Spirit is coming upon Jesus, and Jesus the Son is receiving the Spirit's Baptism and the Father's affirmation. This was a glorious moment. There had to be thousands of people there because people from all of Judea and the entire region around Jordan came to be baptized by John. The masses were hearing the Father's voice from heaven speak delight over his Son. The Father was rewarding him openly for what he had done in secret for the past 30 years. He had pleased the Father in secret and in obscurity and now the Father was declaring it openly and publicly and anointing him for public ministry. Jesus had the most amazing ordination service ever, the Father himself audibly affirming his Son, it doesn't get any better than that. Jesus at thirty years of age entered into his high priestly ministry. The heavens were opened to Jesus, and he saw what the Father was doing. When the heavens are opened, it is so that we can see and hear what he is doing and have a revelation of who Jesus Christ really is and be empowered by the Holy Spirit. Here we see the baptism of the Spirit taking place and Jesus is not speaking in tongues. I am sorry I had to get that one in there. I personally believe the primary purpose of the baptism of the Spirit is to have a revelation of who Jesus Christ truly is. We know by knowledge before by believing the Word, but we come to know by experience as the Baptism of the Spirit takes place. Both are crucial for Biblical learning. *The knowledge before the experience is faith, but the knowledge after the experience matures faith into trust. Trust is faith all grown up.*

In the Gospels, there are three different times where the Father speaks audibly. Out of those three times he only gives one specific directive. We will get into that later so keep reading. Jesus' baptism was the first of the three. All three audible voice encounters that Jesus has with the Father were in context of him being crucified. The disciples did not really want to hear about it; however, the Father seemed to have that topic on his mind every time he spoke audibly in the New Testament. After Jesus' first audible voice encounter, he was led into the wilderness to be tempted by the Devil. Two out of Satan's three temptation attempts were specifically about Jesus' identity as God's Son. The devil said, "If you be the Son of God." The question was not "if" because the Father had just previously declared he was, and so he was. The enemy comes to try to steal our encounter with God's voice because our encounter with his voice causes us to live by his word. It is by the word that the enemy is defeated, so he tries to steal what will defeat him. He failed with Jesus, and we are in him so he will fail with us also but we must not be ignorant of satan's devices. So we must hold onto the Word over our life and live by what God is saying.

The second audible voice encounter Jesus had with the Father was on a mountain with three of his closest friends and two of his old friends. Often times this mountain is referred to as *"the mount of transfiguration."* The mountain was named by what God did on it, not by what a man called it. What God said defined who Jesus was, and what God did defined this mountain. We must get our identity and assignment from what God says. Jesus repeatedly said, *"Take up your cross and follow me."* I guess his disciples did not really get that he was going to the cross. Either they did not have ears to hear or they did not want to hear. The last subject Jesus was talking about before the mount of transfiguration scene was *"losing your life to find it and also his coming."* Then six days later Jesus took Peter, James and John up into a mountain to pray. Matthew 17:2-3 says, *"And was transfigured before them: and his face did shine as the sun, and his raiment was as light."* Paul said, *"We are being changed from glory to glory."* (See 2 Corinthians 3:18.) That concept becomes clearly visible as Jesus begins to pray. Then while Jesus was praying Moses and Elijah appeared, and they talked to Jesus. Jesus was looking for people who would listen to what was on his heart concerning his suffering and death. Luke 9:30-31 says, *"And, behold, there talked with him two men, which were Moses and Elias: Who appeared in glory, and spake of his decease which he should accomplish at Jerusalem."*

So while they were all standing there, Jesus was shining like the sun and Elijah and Moses are talking to him. Then Peter thought of a good idea. He wanted to start a building project. He asked if they want to build three new buildings one for Jesus, one for Elijah and one for Moses. Then the Father spoke.

> *"While he yet spake, behold, a bright cloud overshadowed them: and behold a voice out of the cloud, which said, This is my beloved Son, in whom I am well pleased; hear ye him. And when the disciples heard*

> *it, they fell on their face, and were sore afraid."*
> (Matthew 17:5-6)

Again, we see the Father affirming his Son. Now God is not only affirming his Son but, he is giving a commandment and it is, *"Hear ye him."* This was the only audible directive from the Father in all four Gospels. Perhaps this is the most important thing to him. When someone knows everything and only says one thing, we might want to pay very close attention to what he said. When the Father said, *"Hear ye him,"* he is specifically talking about the subject that Jesus is speaking about that no one wants to hear about. The Father was instructing them to hear or understand what Jesus has been saying that you do not want to hear. The Father was telling them to hear or understand Jesus' death that was coming soon, but they didn't want to hear it. Often God repeats himself because we are not listening or paying attention.

So while these guys were on the floor, Jesus went to them, touched them and said, *"Arise, and be not afraid."* The Father did not even say anything scary and dread fell on them. The passion the Father has for his Son was something beyond measure. This passion brought terror or great fear upon the disciples. Matthew 17:8-9 says, *"And when they had lifted up their eyes, they saw no man, save Jesus only. And as they came down from the mountain, Jesus charged them, saying, Tell the vision to no man, until the Son of man be risen from the dead."* The Father had just told them to hear Jesus and then Jesus immediately tells them not to tell anyone about the vision until he is raised from the dead. All revelation has a specific time as to when it is to be released. *You know the Father is speaking to you when all you can see is Jesus.* The Father has such a passion for Jesus; it is scary, so scary that the disciples ended up on their faces in fear. The Father's passion for Jesus must put us face down in his presence. Often times when someone is face down, his or her ears are open. The easy way to hear God is to cut out all distractions, which is what worship is. It happens when we are completely and solely focused upon God.

As they were going back down the mountain Jesus told them not to tell anyone the vision until after he was raised from the dead. This obviously alludes to the fact that he is going to have to die before he can be raised from the dead. Again, here Jesus is speaking of what the Father specifically just told them to hear, which is his death. Revelation is not ours but it's his, which is why the revelation must also be released in his timing. They had a seeing and hearing encounter with God, but they still had to hear his voice as to when this revelation could be released. *Hearing God is crucial even when it comes to seeing visions and having dreams.* Without hearing his voice, a dream or a vision is still incomplete. It was not enough to hear the Father audibly or see Jesus' face shine like the sun; they still needed to hear when this revelation could be shared with those who needed to hear it. It is evident that Jesus wanted them to share the vision, *"but not until he was risen from the dead."* Sharing this vision with others may give them ears to hear. The Father desires that we hear his Son. The Father did not give us Jesus just so he could die for us; he also gave Jesus to us so that we can live by what he is saying, and so he can live his life through us as we hear and obey him. We draw near to him to hear him. All the paper in the world could not fully communicate the Father's desire for us to hear his Son.

Before Jesus' third audible voice encounter with the Father, he preached this amazing message. The message was so good that some of his followers stopped following him! Sometimes the response of the masses has nothing to do with how good a message or minister really is. *Often times the masses do not have ears to ear.* However, in this hour I believe the Lord wants to equip his people to hear his voice and follow him. As we hear his voice and follow him, we have access to his power and resources, so that his kingdom would come and his will would be done. Best of all, we get to know him intimately as we hear and obey. Our intimacy with Jesus is as deep as our obedience to Jesus. John 6:53 says, *"Then Jesus said unto them, Verily, verily, I say unto you, Except ye eat the flesh of the Son of man, and drink his blood, ye have no life in you."* This was not a seeker sensitive, watered down message. Jesus did not give a rip if people did not understand him; he simply heard the Father and said what he heard. This was a radical message to the Jews because eating people was against the law and in the natural this was a sin. However, Jesus was not speaking in the natural he was speaking in the Spirit. Perhaps this is why the Apostle Paul said, *"that natural man does not receive the things of the Spirit."* What he was saying was, *"If you do not receive my sacrifice you have no life and will have no life in the age to come."* Again, we hear Jesus referring to his sacrifice. This message was taught right in the synagogue of Capernaum. Jesus was not *"tolerant or relevant"* but he did love his Father enough to say what he was saying in spite of the responses he would get from people. In Colossians 1:9, Paul prayed that the Colossians would have spiritual understanding. Unfortunately, that is what these people were lacking.

After Jesus had said this, some of his disciple's murmured, and then he asked them, *"Doth this offend you?"* Jesus has the most amazing personality. Often people are offended at what they do not understand. This is a sign of spiritual immaturity. I am sure you or I have never been offended at something we do not understand, haha. It's ok to laugh while you read this book. Faith comes by hearing and understanding comes through faith according to Hebrews 11:3. Jesus continued his discourse by speaking about his ascension. Then he said something profound. John 6:63 says, *"It is the spirit that quickeneth; the flesh profiteth nothing: the words that I speak unto you, they are spirit, and they are life."* After that many of his disciples walked with him no more. He lost followers because they stopped believing what they did not understand, instead of knowing that faith will mature them into understanding. The message of the cross cost Jesus many of his disciples, and the cross cost Jesus his life. After the many disciples leave, he turned to the few left and said, *"Will you go away also?"* Then Peter turned to him and said, *"Lord, to whom shall we go? You have the words of eternal life. And we believe and are sure that you are the Christ, the Son of the Living God."* (Matthew 16:16) They did not understand his last message, but they understood who he was by the words he spoke. It was not just what he did, but it was also by what he said. What we say and what we do, reveal who we really are. Not performance based identity, but identity based performance. Jesus didn't die to prove he was the Son of God, but he died and rose because he was the Son of God. The few disciples that were still with Jesus did not allow what they did not understand to keep them from following the one they loved and put their faith in.

After Jesus was anointed for burial, and after he came into Jerusalem on a young donkey, he goes back into his message of the cross.

> *"Verily, verily, I say unto you, Except a corn of wheat fall into the ground and die, it abideth alone: but if it die, it bringeth forth much fruit. He that loveth his life shall lose it; and he that hateth his life in this world shall keep it unto life eternal. If any man serve me, let him follow me; and where I am, there shall also my servant be: if any man serve me, him will my Father honor. Now is my soul troubled; and what shall I say? Father, save me from this hour: but for this cause came I unto this hour. Father, glorify thy name. Then came there a voice from heaven, saying, I have both glorified it, and will glorify it again. The people therefore, that stood by, and heard it, said that it thundered: others said, An angel spake to him. Jesus answered and said, This voice came not because of me, but for your sakes. Now is the judgment of this world: now shall the prince of this world be cast out. And I, if I be lifted up from the earth, will draw all men unto me."* (John 12:24-32)

This is the third time Jesus heard the audible voice of the Father and all three times they are related to his crucifixion. Before and after the audible voice of the Father, Jesus began and ended with the message of his death. Yet, the disciples did not want to hear it. I am sure we are not like that at all. In immaturity we follow Jesus for what we can get, as we mature and get to know him and we become like him and we are in it for what we can give.

If God is speaking to us about something repeatedly he is taking us deeper and drawing us closer. Another reason for him to repeat himself is simply because we are not paying attention. Often God will repeat what we don't want to hear so that we have a change of heart and mind. In his goodness and patience God does this to align us with his very will. Hearing the message of his death meant that they were going to have to die to their ambitions that were rooted in their bad eschatology. That is a whole other story and we will save that for later. Sometimes there are things that we believe that are false and they hinder us from being able to hear the truth. The crowd around Jesus was divided by what they heard. Some thought it was thunder and others thought it was an angel, but what is funny is they were both wrong. *What is scary is without the mind of Christ you cannot hear God even if he speaks audibly.* From the Garden until this present day, people have been divided over what God has said or what he is saying. It is time we hear him and get unified with the head of the body. The word sanctifies and the Spirit unifies. Let's get on the same page with Jesus and one another. To you it has been given to know the mysteries of the Kingdom. Those mysteries are received by seeing and hearing, and I speak over you the very words of Jesus, *"Blessed are your eyes that see and your ears that hear."*

Questions

1. Has God repeatedly spoken to you about something you don't want to hear about?

2. Do you change the subject on God without listening to him? If so ask him to forgive you and be willing to listen to him and obey.

Prayer

Father, in Jesus name I ask you to help us to hear the things we do not want to hear, so we can become the people you want us to be.

Chapter 7
The Posture of Humility

H*umility makes us irresistible to God.* One day I was praying and Jesus said to me, *"Adam, I am going to teach you how to be irresistible to the Father just like I AM."* What he was saying was I am going to teach you humility. This just may have meant that I was not the most humble character, not like coming from an Italian family from New Jersey might have anything to do with that. James 4:6 says, *"But he giveth more grace. Wherefore he saith, God resisteth the proud, but giveth grace unto the humble."*

One of the ways God resists someone is by not speaking to that person. In the Old Testament, Saul had to try to wake Samuel from the dead by divination because he could not hear from God. The reason he could not hear from God is because he was proud, and God was resisting him. Many people in church say I am waiting on God and some people are, but what just may be happening is that they are proud and God is waiting on them to humble themselves so he does not have to resist someone he really loves and desires to speak to. The more we submit to God the more we will hear from God. The result of humility is a tender heart that will cause our will to be surrendered and are ears to be opened.

To effectively advance the Kingdom through the preaching of the Gospel, we must hear God and move with him. When we are humble, we are teachable. When someone is teachable, God loves to speak to that person. Humility allows us to see clearly in the spirit. *We need to be clothed with humility so we can walk in revelation without being proud.* Knowledge puffs up while true revelation of Jesus will cause us to bow low. *Authentic ministry is always preceded by revelation.* One of the things I learned early in my walk with God is that it is far more important for me to shut up and hear what he is saying than to tell him something he already knows I need in his name. We live by what he says; he does not live by what we say. Therefore we need to remember that when we pray. I am not belittling our petitions I am simply focusing our prayers more on listening to him, instead of him listening to us. The posture of humility will allow us to receive what we need from the Lord. Humility knows what is the first priority. Humility is not just being quiet; it knows when to speak and when to be quiet.

Jesus just finished explaining to a lawyer what eternal life looks like. Now he is headed to Martha's house for a meal.

> *"Now it came to pass, as they went, that he entered into a certain village: and a certain woman named Martha received him into her house."* (Luke 10:38)

In those days the house would be named after the husband who was the head of the house, so either Martha is a widow and her husband died or she never had a husband. That is just a little bit of culture. Let us continue to see the story unfold.

> *"And she had a sister called Mary, which also sat at Jesus' feet, and heard his word. But Martha was cumbered about much serving, and came to him, and said, Lord, dost thou not care that my sister hath left me to serve alone? Bid her therefore that she help me. And Jesus answered and said unto her, Martha, Martha, thou art careful and troubled about many things: But one thing is needful: and Mary hath chosen that good part, which shall not be taken away from her."* (Luke 10:39-42)

The description of where Mary is sitting reveals a lot about her. Her posture is one of great humility; she is in a low place. Mary, in proximity, is very close to Jesus. Meaning if she is at Jesus' feet no one is coming between Jesus and her.

When the scripture said, *"She sat at Jesus' feet to hear his word."* That had some cultural relevance to those it was written to, which should be understood to grasp the depth of her posture before the Lord. Many times revelation comes from knowledge, and other times revelation brings about knowledge. In proximity and humility you can never go wrong. Humility will bring about proximity, meaning if you are humble you will be close to the Lord simply because he is not resisting you. Therefore, he will draw near to you as you draw near to him. There is nothing better than that. Here is another example of the concept of being at someone's feet. This is Paul the Apostle speaking here in Acts 22:3, *"I am verily a man which am a Jew, born in Tarsus, a city in Cilicia, yet brought up in this city at the feet of Gamaliel, and taught according to the perfect manner of the law of the fathers, and was zealous toward God, as ye are this day."* When Paul mentioned *"at his feet"* he is referring to submitting to Gamaliel's teaching and being under his authority. This woman, Mary, was not just hungry to hear God's voice she came under his the authority of Jesus. Her decision will pay off in then end. We will see later as her story unfolds. She recognized who Jesus was and positioned herself properly.

I do not really want to make Martha look bad, seeing that she is not here to defend herself. However, I want to show you that accusation is the fruit of not hearing God. Martha was not paying attention to what Jesus was saying and so she was accusing Mary. Mary did not have time to accuse Martha of not listening to Jesus because she was listening to Jesus, which meant she was not thinking about Martha. *When our attention is focused in the wrong place, often times wrong things come out of our mouths.* Jesus graciously and truthfully responded to her by giving her his perspective on the whole situation. He first addressed her anxiety and worry about many things that were being suppressed as she served. Then he told her what Mary was doing was right and what the results would be. Jesus did not compare Mary and Martha; he compared their decisions in the present situation.

Here was Jesus' response to Martha concerning Mary. Luke 10:42 says, *"But one thing is needful: and Mary hath chosen that good part, which shall not be taken away from her."* There are several things to receive from this, one being Jesus was not afraid to confront someone's foolishness. Also, he becomes Mary's advocate because she did not try to defend herself or justify herself. Truly Jesus was her justification. He said one thing is *"needful."* The word *needful* literally means *employment, requirement and necessary.* Mary chose well, and so we must follow her example. We too must sit at Jesus' feet and hear his word. There is a mystery revealed here concerning the Word. The thief comes to steal the word, but in *humility and in proximity he cannot.* Mary positioned herself so close to Jesus that no one could get in between her and him, including the thief. Martha could not get between her and Jesus and neither could the enemy. When we do not feel the need to defend ourselves Jesus does, and when he is present, the enemy cannot operate in any authoritative role. We must remember to never let any one or their opinions of us get in between Jesus and us. Mary positioned herself in such a way that the word could not be taken from her. *Humility disarms the enemy and causes Jesus, our advocate and defender, to rise up and fight for us.* Mary will later do a great exploit because she sat at Jesus' feet and heard his word. She is the only one that scripture refers to in that she, *"sat at his feet and heard his Word"* or *Logos* in Greek. *Logos* is the Word used in John 1 when it says, *"In the beginning was the Word." Logos*, in Greek, is referring to Jesus himself. He revealed himself to her because she sat down to hear him. Humility causes us to hear God and God's love for us causes him to reveal himself to us. *Love and humility work together to form a true Christian. A Christian is formed as Christ speaks.* As He speaks the word to us He is formed in us.

Before the Passover, Jesus returned to Bethany. Martha was serving dinner, Lazarus was at the table with Jesus and Mary once again was at his feet. This time she was not just listening but she was now acting because she had previously listened. Before Martha was offended at Mary's ability to tune into Jesus and tune the rest of the world out. Now her love will uncover other people's bad values and spiritual blindness.

> *"Then Mary took a pound of ointment of spikenard, very costly, and anointed the feet of Jesus, and wiped his feet with her hair: and the house was filled with the odor of the ointment."*
> (John 12:3)

Mary truly chose what would not be taken from her as Jesus said because she anointed Jesus for burial. He was only going to die once and she had the privilege of anointing him for the very purpose he came—to die. This was the greatest honor. This perhaps was the greatest thing a human ever did for Jesus throughout the ages. Wherever the Gospel goes, this story is told as a memorial for her according to Matthew 26:13. *She sat at his feet to hear his word. There her eyes were opened and she saw the cross before him and anointed him for burial.*

Mary saw what no one else saw because she had ears to hear. In learning to listen we are actually being trained by God to see in the Spirit. Jesus continually spoke to his disciples about the cross, yet they did not want to hear it. They did not see because they were not listening which mean that they were not hearing or understanding. Our spiritual eyes are opened as we learn to hear God. *Our ability to hear God will determine our ability to see what he is doing.* Judas the betrayer was offended by her love offering; he wanted to give the money to the poor or steal it perhaps? Jesus told them, *"The poor you will always have with you, but me you will not always have."* True worship is offensive to people whose hearts are not right with God. Worship was not just Mary pouring out the oil on Jesus' feet. Worship was also her sitting at Jesus' feet to hear his word. Although Mary never confronted anyone, her love and devotion to Jesus naturally confronted people. Our love for Jesus will draw a line in the sand and people will either love him and us or hate him and us.

It just messes me up when I think of what Mary did. The Father spoke audibly to the disciples on the mount of transfiguration by saying, *"hear him"* and she did. Imagine what the Father felt when he saw this woman anointing his Son to carry out his plan. What was the Father feeling? What the Father was feeling was so deep and strong that the Son said, *"Wherever this Gospel shall be preached in the whole world, this story shall be told as a memorial to her"* (paraphrased). The Father liked what she did enough to have her story told wherever Jesus is preached. All of this happened because she had ears to hear and she was willing to invest herself in what she heard. Her reward will not be taken from her because Jesus prophesied that wherever the Gospel goes so will her story. None of his words fall to the ground and what he says you can count on.

What is really interesting is that no where in scripture does it tell us that Jesus asked her or told her to do this. When he revealed himself to her, she just knew whom he was and what he was going to do. When we get revelation of Jesus, it begins to define our purpose. *Our purpose unfolds as he reveals himself.* Do not worry about your purpose in life; make his voice your number one priority and your purpose will be clear even if he does not mention it to you audibly. Several times in the Bible people did amazing exploits that scripture does not record God telling them to do. For example, God never told David to kill Goliath, but it was in his heart because he loved God. As we cultivate ears to hear, our hearts begin to feel, and we begin to intuitively know what God wants even if he does not say it specifically. I have this kind of relationship with my wife. When we go to a restaurant and I am in the bathroom and the waiter comes over to take our drink order she knows exactly what I want without me even telling her. Sarah knows me; therefore, she knows what I want. The Father desires our relationship with Jesus to grow into this same kind of knowledge. Paul prayed a prayer for the Colossians and in it he mentioned that they would be *"Filled with the knowledge of his will."* We become filled with the knowledge of his will as we read his word and hear his voice. His will is attached to his word; his word is formed as his voice is heard. Even when he is not talking we can hear him because he has given us the mind of Christ.

Thoughts to Remember

1. If God resists the proud and gives grace to the humble, we must stay humble and we will never struggle to hear God speak.

2. Keeping our hearts tender means our will is surrendered and our ears are opened.

3. God reveals himself to us and that revelation of him begins to define our purpose.

Prayer

Father, help me to learn humility. I want to walk humbly with you. As I walk with you reveal yourself to me and reveal your very purpose for my life. Help me to do those things that are pleasing in your sight. I ask these things in Jesus name.

Chapter 8
Creating a Sustainable Atmosphere Where God Can Continually Speak

When we remember what God has done, it is easy to hear what he is saying. When we value what he says, we obey him and he manifests himself. As we learn to value what he has said, it helps us to hear what he is saying. Remembering what God has said shows him we value him and what he says, which makes him want to speak to the person or people who listen and remember. When we remember, we stay tender. One of the ways we guard our heart is by remembering what God has said and done. God knows therefore he speaks; we need to learn; therefore, we must cultivate ears to hear. Listening precedes learning the same way hearing precedes obeying. Listening is a learned behavior, but it is priceless once it is acquired.

The Father's main priority is that we hear his Son and obey him. We must not only be hearers of the word.

> *"But be ye doers of the word, and not hearers only, deceiving your ownselves."* (James 1:22)

One of the ways to be deceived is to know the truth and not do anything with it. We can have sound doctrine and be completely deceived. Truth is meant to be experienced. We experience truth as we hear God and obey him. The Holy Spirit leads us into all truth. We are his temple and as his temple we must learn to create an atmosphere that is pleasing to him. If we are his temple, it means he is in charge. We are his temple; we are his possession; therefore, we must keep the temple clean and pure. When Jesus came to the earth and saw that people had made his Father's house like a market, he made a whip and went in and physically got people out. That is what we must do with our sin and the issues in our life that are polluting God's temple. The more we are sanctified the easier it becomes to hear God's voice. Often the majority of people that struggle with hearing God's voice have not made the choice to be sanctified from the world for the purpose of Kingdom advancement. The Kingdom advances as God speaks, so we must learn to listen. One of the greatest expressions of love and honor is listening. Listening is one of the most costly skills to learn because we have to be intentional about staying focused and being quiet in order to learn to listen. Love listens and hears. It takes a humble person to hear. The continual process of listening is what makes us willing because as we hear we are empowered to obey. The heart of humility is the posture of listening, which is the positioning for hearing. Our posture and positioning will determine what we will and will not receive from the Lord.

As we learn to listen and wait on God, there is a specific way that we should wait. We should wait with hope, patience and in peace.

"Rest in the Lord, and wait patiently for him: fret not thyself because of him who prospereth in his way, because of the man who bringeth wicked devices to pass." (Psalm 37:7)

In this scripture, rest means to be silent and hold peace, be still or quiet self. One of the ways we learn to hear God is by turning self off. We are crucified with Christ so we can hear his voice and live a resurrected life of faithfulness and obedience. Meaning when we shut up, we give the Lord an opportunity to speak up and he certainly will. The simplicity of understanding that Jesus loves us and wants to speak to us must take hold of us fully if we are going to know him and serve him wholly and boldly.

The lesson of peace and rest is seen in two amazing stories, and I will reference them both due to the importance of us learning to be at peace. As we learn to be at peace, we will learn to hear God speak.

> "And Moses went up into the mount, and a cloud covered the mount. And the glory of the Lord abode upon mount Sinai, and the cloud covered it six days: and the seventh day he called unto Moses out of the midst of the cloud." (Exodus 24:15-16)

This is a great picture of waiting patiently. Moses went up the mountain and he drew near to God, and God drew near to him. Here we see a clear picture of what James said, *"If you draw near to God, he will draw near to you."* When he draws near to us it is because he plans on speaking to us. Moses was in God's manifested glory presence for six days and God was completely silent. On the seventh day or on the day of rest God spoke. God speaks from the place of rest; we can hear God clearly when we are at peace. Peace is not determined by our circumstances, and rest is not determined by our day off. Rest and peace is a privileged position that we have as children of God because of the cross of Christ. To have a real value for peace we must deeply understand how much it cost. How much someone will pay for something determines what it is worth.

> *"But he was wounded for our transgressions, he was bruised for our iniquities: the chastisement of our peace was upon him; and with his stripes we are healed."* (Isaiah 53:5) Jesus was tortured so that we could have peace. He valued our spiritual peace enough to be physically tortured. Here he gave us beauty for ashes. He exchanged the beauty of his peace for the ashes of our confusion, worry, anxiety and fear. This is an amazing deal. He was not just tortured to purchase peace for us. He was tortured so his peace would be imparted to us, so he himself would be our peace. Jesus was not buying peace from a vendor, for he is our peace. When we abide in him, we do not just have peace but he is our peace. The atmosphere Jesus lived in during his life on the earth is the atmosphere we must live in as he abides in us and we abide in him. If we are abiding in him, we are hearing him clearly and consistently.

Jesus and his disciples went for a small boat ride. Before they left Jesus said, *"Let us pass over to the other side."* So Jesus decided to take a snooze. While he was sleeping, a great storm emerged.

The disciples woke Jesus up accusing him of not caring about them. Many times we do this. We start accusing Jesus any time calamity or hard times come. When they forgot what God had said, they became vulnerable to the accuser of the brethren, the devil himself. When we forget what Jesus said, often we lose our peace. If he is our peace and we forget what he said, we may possibly lose our peace. Although the devil is not mentioned in this passage, there were some "false accusations" that certainly did not come from God. The disciples threw "false accusations" at Jesus because their circumstances were dictating their atmosphere. So Jesus dealt with their immaturity and the storm.

Mark 4:39 says, *"And he arose, and rebuked the wind, and said unto the sea, Peace, be still. And the wind ceased, and there was a great calm."* Jesus only said what he heard the Father saying, and he only did what he saw the Father do. The Father's voice is what controlled the Son's internal atmosphere. Circumstances did not control Jesus rather he changed circumstances by maintaining his peace. Peace is clearly more powerful than the storm. We can only speak to the storm we can sleep in, meaning we have authority against what we do not lose our peace to. Jesus had peace, so he could release it. Jesus' words and actions were in agreement; this is how we are to live. We can only give what we have. In order to give, we must first receive. Rest and peace positions us to receive from the Father.

Jesus was fully man so he had to sleep. He was fully God so he could sleep in a storm. I personally think Jesus said to his disciples, "Let us pass over to the other side," so that word could guard their hearts from the fear of the storm. However, when they failed to remember, they lost their peace. In this story Jesus' peace passed all understanding. If our peace does not pass understanding, we need more peace. Peace is not the absence of problems or conflicts; it is a choice to trust God fully in the midst of them. In peace we receive what we could not earn by striving. Jesus was tortured for our peace; therefore, we must hold onto it and value it because of the great price he paid to freely give it to us.

Romans 14:17 says, *"For the Kingdom of God is not meat nor drink; but righteousness, peace and joy in the Holy Ghost."* Everyone in the Kingdom of God has been made righteous by the blood of Jesus Christ. Peace and joy is the atmosphere of the Kingdom because it is the atmosphere of the King. That is also our atmosphere when King Jesus is ruling and reigning in our hearts and minds. In that atmosphere, God's voice is clearly heard. In that atmosphere, it is easy to hear God. When we have trouble hearing God it could be that our focus is elsewhere. When God's voice becomes unclear, it may be because things that really do not matter have polluted our affections. When our priorities are out of order, it also may be hard to hear God. However, God's priorities are that he speaks to us and we listen and obey him. The will of God is that we would hear and obey him, that is simple and we should keep it that way.

Paul the Apostle lays out the will of God for the Thessalonians in a marvelous yet very simple way. When he does this, he lays out a simple pattern that creates an atmosphere that is conducive to God speaking. When this really got a hold of me, I realized it really did not matter what was going on, on the outside. What is more important is what is going on in the inside. We are seated with Christ in heavenly places; therefore, we must live from heaven towards earth. That is why Jesus said, *"On earth as it is in heaven."* According to Jesus, *"The kingdom of God is within."* Therefore, we must live from the inside out. Most people, including many believers, live from the outside in. This is a recipe for disaster. When our circumstances determine how we feel, is Jesus really our Lord or are our circumstances our Lord at the moment? Once and a while we need to have a reality check.

Here is Paul's simplistic yet highly profound revelation of the will of God. Remember God is attracted to his will. This means that God is thoroughly present in his will. His will is not a bunch of do's and don'ts, but it is God interacting with us, so that we become like him and bring people to him in the process. His will involves his voice, presence and power.

> *"Rejoice always. Pray without ceasing. In everything give thanks: for this is the will of God in Christ Jesus concerning you. Quench not the Spirit. Despise not prophesying."*
> (1 Thessalonians 5:16-20)

Joy is just simply empowering. "For the joy set before Jesus he endured the cross." "The joy of the Lord is our strength." (See Hebrews 12:2 & Nehemiah 8:10) We approach God's will with his strength, empowered to become and fulfill what he desires. Rejoicing is what happens when there is an abundance of joy. In Christ, we are called to abundance. We are called to live in his Kingdom and there is no lack there. The reality of the Kingdom should affect how we live, especially if we say that we are walking in the truth. In the Kingdom of God there is no competition because there is no lack. When this reality touches us it affects how we feel, see and treat others. We would not be able to rejoice always if God was not always in a good mood. I just want to stop and let you know that Jesus is in an amazing mood today and forever.

Pray without ceasing. This describes Jesus' relationship with the Father. Paul gets this statement from Luke 18:1 when it says, "men always ought to pray, and not to faint." There was a continual flow between the Father and the Son through the inward counsel of the Precious Holy Spirit in the place of prayer. The audible voice encounters that Jesus had with the Father were not really ministry directives but more personal affirmations of a purpose he already was very clear about. Also, consider that he was the Lamb slain from before the foundation of the world. Almost everything Jesus did was through the inward counsel of the Holy Spirit. We have been given the same Holy Spirit that led Jesus. Praying in the Spirit is another key to hearing God's voice. If you speak his language, he will speak yours. The principle of sowing and reaping also pertains to our relationship with God.

> *"For he that speaketh in an unknown tongue speaketh not unto men, but unto God: for no man understandeth him; howbeit in the spirit he speaketh mysteries. Jesus said, To you it has been given to*

know the mysteries of the Kingdom." (1 Corinthians 14:2)

The mysteries of the Kingdom are released when the King speaks that is why listening and hearing is so important. We can pray in tongues for days and make a huge deposit in our mystery account in heaven, but if we do not listen it becomes hard for him to reveal things to us if we are not paying attention to him.

"Let a man so account of us, as of the ministers of Christ, and the stewards of the mysteries of God." (1 Corinthians 4:1) We are to steward the mysteries of the Kingdom that we have received by hearing God. Prayer is a two-way conversation between us and God, and what he can say to us if far more valuable than what we can say to him because he already knows what we are going to say before we speak.

In all things give thanks. Psalm 100:4 says, *"Enter into his gates with thanksgiving, and into his courts with praise: be thankful unto him, and bless his name."* When we come near to God, there is thanksgiving in the outer courts, praise in the Holy Place and worship in the most Holy Place. This ordered process begins with thanksgiving. It is not only about giving thanks, but it's also about living continually thankful. Thanksgiving gives us access to the supernatural. Jesus was standing before thousands of hungry people. He lifted up the bread to his Father, gave thanks, broke it and passed it to his disciples to pass out to the people. The giving of thanks opened the realm of the miraculous. Jesus was thankful in the lack of their natural situation and the abundance of his Kingdom was manifested. One of the doors into the supernatural realms of God's power and provision is thanksgiving. We enter into his gates with thanksgiving. Gates speak of authority; we have access to Jesus' authority through thanksgiving because he had access to his Father's provision through thanksgiving. Thanksgiving will either produce a testimony or make us the testimony. Thanksgiving will keep us in God's presence even when our circumstances are not favorable at the moment. Thanksgiving is a sustainable reality for all who live in the Kingdom. There is no complaining in the Kingdom of God. Giving thanks is the will of God in Christ Jesus concerning you.

Quench not the Spirit. Despise not prophesying. As we are empowered by joy, we stay in the place of continual prayer. Jesus' atmosphere and our atmosphere become one despite our circumstances. This will keep us very grateful and thankful. To be in a never-ending conversation with God is the highest privilege of all. Paul goes from being thankful to, *"quench not the Spirit"* because he knew the Holy Spirit is attracted to thanksgiving. Then he goes from, *"quench not the Spirit"* to, *"Despise not prophesying"* because when the Holy Spirit comes often times prophecy comes with him. Remember the Holy Spirit is the Spirit of Prophecy. The Holy Spirit does not come empty handed; he comes with gifts according to his will. Paul the apostle lays out how to create an atmosphere of intimacy, which gives birth to prophecy. Prophecy should flow from intimacy. Prophecy is necessary for Kingdom advancement because nothing happens in the Kingdom without declaration. When the King speaks, we echo what he is saying and he begins to manifest his will as we partner with his word. For us to do this continually we must create an internal atmosphere that is conducive to his voice. This is made possible through the Holy Spirit who dwells inside.

We must choose to be peaceful, prayerful, thankful and joyful. When we make this choice he gives us the grace to walk it out. We must make the choice not to be defiled within and he will give us the grace to walk it out.

> *"But Daniel purposed in his heart that he would not defile himself with the portion of the king's meat, nor with the wine which he drank: therefore he requested of the prince of the eunuchs that he might defile himself. Now God had brought Daniel into favor and tender love with the prince of the eunuchs."*
> (Daniel 1:8-9)

Take note when it says *"but Daniel"* and *"Now God."* Daniel made a choice to honor God, and God brought Daniel into a place of favor so he could walk out his decision. We must understand our part in God's will. Daniel made one decision, and he had to make choices to affirm his decision. That is how it is with us. We cannot do God's job, and he will not do our job. We must make one decision and many right choices to walk that decision out. Remember you can do it because God has put his grace towards you so you can put your faith in him. When his grace touches your faith the miraculous is activated. Remember you are his sheep, and you do hear his voice.

Thoughts to Remember

1. Remember the will of God is on the inside. When the inside is in order your steps will be ordered also.

2. Thanksgiving creates an atmosphere conducive to God speaking and gives us access to the supernatural realms of God's power, wisdom and provision.

Prayer

Father, I ask you to set my life in order. Would you clearly reveal your will to me so that I may do what is pleasing and acceptable to you. It's in Jesus name that I pray Father.

Chapter 9
The Mind of Christ

Since we are his sheep and we hear his voice, the question is where do we hear his voice? Often times you will hear people say, *"The Lord spoke to my heart."* My question is was he speaking to your left ventricle or your right atrium? For those of you who do not know, those are different parts of the human heart. It is very clear that he is not talking to our left ventricle or our right atrium. What people are really referring to when they say that God spoke to their "heart" are usually their affections. The predominant way we hear God is in our mind, or rather his mind. That is why we have been given the mind of Christ. *We have been given the mind of Christ so that we can hear God even when he is silent.*

There is either the carnal mind, which is at enmity with God, or the renewed mind that proves the will of God. *The carnal mind cannot hear God because it is at war with him.* The renewed mind is such a big deal; it will determine whether we will hear God or not. The carnal mind opposes God's thoughts that are in us. The carnal mind discredits the thoughts that we have that are *"God thoughts."* The vaccination for the carnal mind is the word of God.

> *"For the word of God is quick and powerful, sharper than any two-edged sword, piercing even to the dividing asunder of the soul and spirit, and of the joints and marrow, and is a discerner of the thoughts and the intents of the heart."* (Hebrews 4:12)

If the word of God is a discerner of the thoughts and the intents of the heart, God obviously speaks to us in our renewed mind. When the word of God is in us, we discern or judge the thoughts that come to us by the Holy Spirit administrating the word to the thoughts, intents and even the circumstances. The word discerns the thoughts and the intents. Here is a brief example. The thoughts would be "what" we want to do, and the intents would be "why" we want to do what we want to do. The word clearly helps us to hear and see in the Spirit because the Word of God is Spirit. *"And take the helmet of salvation, and the sword of the Spirit, which is the word of God:"* (Ephesians 6:17). Again we see no separation between the Word the Spirit.

I would like to make a New Testament / Old Testament parallel and then go deeper into the mind of Christ. The *converted soul* of the *Old Testament* is the *renewed mind* of the *New Testament*. God renews our mind so we can think his thoughts. He converts and restores our soul so it can be the painting board that perceives, proves and clearly sees his will.

"The law of the Lord is perfect, converting the soul: the testimony of the Lord is sure, making wise the simple." (Psalm 19:7)

The testimony of what the Lord has done is usually manifested through someone with a converted soul. The Law converts the soul to believe God's word. *In the obedience to God's word, his power is accessible to his people, to produce a testimony.* The testimony brings glory to him. The testimony of the Lord will turn a fool into a wise man if he will only believe enough to obey. The soul is restored as we believe the word and obey. Believing and obeying the word is what will produce the testimonies, which turn fools into wise men.

Here is the New Testament parallel of the converted soul. Romans 12:2 says, *"And be not conformed to this world: but be ye transformed by the renewing of your mind, that ye may prove what is the good, and acceptable, and perfect, will of God."* The renewed mind is able to see and perceive the will of God. Paul goes on to tell the Romans that they should not think more highly of themselves than they ought to; he also tells them to think soberly. The renewed mind causes us to see who we really are and who we are really not. The renewed mind affects how we see, and what we think about.

In the natural world our eyes do not tell us what we are seeing, our brain does. Our eyes send an invisible signal to our brain and our brain converts that signal and tells us what we are seeing. That is why we have been given the mind of Christ so that we can see from his perspective. His perspective is necessary if we are going to live out his dream for our lives.

It is necessary to see the mind of Christ in action and see its potential to take us into the very purpose of why we are even breathing. Before Jesus was crucified he prayed in the Garden.

> *"Saying, Father, if thou be willing, remove this cup from me: nevertheless not my will, but thine, be done. And there appeared an angel unto him from heaven, strengthened him. And being in agony he prayed more earnestly: and his sweat was as it were great drops of blood falling to the ground. And when he rose up from prayer, and was come to his disciples, he found them sleeping for sorrow."* (Luke 22:42-45)

There is so much in these few verses. One thing that is really interesting is that the Father sends an angel that Jesus created to help strengthen him. Here his divinity and humanity is clearly visible. The creation is assisting and serving the creator in fulfilling his purpose. Jesus was strengthened to die. The Father did not audibly speak to Jesus in this scripture, so it was the mind of Christ that perceived the will of God in the place of earnest prayer. When we are praying, we must not discredit the thoughts of our mind because we have been given the mind of Christ. Often we discredit God's thoughts in our mind and then say to him, *"Lord I want to hear your voice."* I can *imagine* the Father smiling and saying, *"I have given you the mind of Christ so you can and are, now just believe."* Someone who does not believe what God has previously said will have real trouble hearing what he is saying. *Someone who has believed what God has said will be able to hear what God is saying. We are supposed to live by what God is saying.* Therefore, hearing God is a life or death situation of the utmost importance.

Jesus said to satan in Matthew 4:4, *"It is written, man shall not live by bread alone, but by every word that proceedeth out of the mouth of God."* The written scriptures are completely necessary if we are going to clearly hear and discern the proceeding word of God. Jesus, who is the word, referenced the scriptures when talking to the devil himself. *When the fear of the Lord is lost, the reverence for the scriptures is lost with it.* This can be a great tragedy especially within the Charismatic movement in which I am a part of. *The fear of the Lord values nothing above God's presence and word.* We are supposed to live in his presence, as his word is a lamp unto our feet and a light unto our path. Beloved, his word is a lamp unto our feet and a light unto our path because we are supposed to follow Jesus into the darkness and let our lights so shine before men so that they glorify the Father because of what we do. The Lamp would be the written scriptures or the *"logos"* Word and the Light would be the voice of God that is heard from the proceeding or the *"rhema"* word. Scripture is what teaches us what God's voice is like. In Daniel 10:21, the glorified Jesus came to speak to Daniel about the *"scripture of truth,"* In Luke 24, the resurrected Jesus came to speak to two of his disciples about himself from the Law, the Prophets and the Psalms. Generally speaking, when we are not reading the Bible and God is talking to you about the Bible, it is Jesus speaking, unless it is the Holy Spirit reminding you of what Jesus previously revealed or said. We will get further into discerning the voice of the Father, Son and Holy Spirit later in this book.

When Jesus was in the garden of Gethsemane praying, he began to pray more earnestly. After his intensity increased, he began to bleed. Perhaps he began to bleed because *"the life of the flesh is in the blood"* and *"man lives by every word that proceeds from the mouth of God"* and when the Father stopped speaking, the Son started bleeding? (See Leviticus 17:11) When the Father did not respond after the more earnest prayer, Jesus gathered his answer from what the Father had previously said. It was the mind of Christ that navigated Jesus' understanding to remember the very purpose of his coming. Often times the answer we are searching for is in us because we have the mind of Christ. We must simply ask the Holy

Spirit to bring to our remembrance that which he has promised or purposed for us to do. Sometimes to determine purpose and judgment, a verdict or decision must be made. The mind of Christ judges righteously and can execute justice and can make important decisions in a split second. The mind of Christ is naturally supernatural; it is simply who he is. 1 Corinthians 2:16 says, *"For who hath known the Lord, that he may instruct him? But we have the mind of Christ."* The mind of Christ allows us to hear God when he is silent and to clearly see his will.

What we focus on is what or whom we will hear from. In the natural world, if we are in a room and there are a lot of people talking, sometimes it is hard to hear the person or persons we are conversing with. However, if we are really interested in and focused upon the conversation we are having, we still hear what is being said. So our interest determines our focus, and our focus determines our willingness to keep this very important conversation going. This is just like our relationship with Jesus. *If we focus on him, it is easy to hear from him.* However, if we focus on our circumstances or ourselves then we will hear from our circumstances and ourselves. We can't focus on our circumstances and wonder why we don't hear from God. Instead we should focus on *Jesus, what he is saying to us and what he is saying about our circumstances. What we meditate on is what we become like and what we premeditate is what we will do.* The Bible tells us to meditate on the Law of God day and night because the Law converts our souls so that we do what is right. We are also told to meditate on the law day and night because Jesus fulfilled the law and as we meditate on it he reveals himself and empowers us to live an overcoming life in him. This is so God can command a blessing to all those who obey him.

In Psalm 19, David reveals something in prayer form. Later in the scriptures, Paul mentions something very similar to David's prayer that very well may be an answer to what David was praying. *"Let the words of my mouth, and the meditations of my heart, be acceptable in thy sight, O Lord, my strength and my redeemer."*
(Psalm 19:14)

Nothing is hidden from the eyes of the Lord; he can even see what we think. When the meditations of our heart are right, the words of our mouth are right also. Usually what we meditate on or think about is what we speak about also. As we fast-forward in time to at least 2,000 years later, Paul tells the Philippians what to think about which will directly affect their actions. Generally speaking, our thoughts direct our words and our words often direct our actions.

> Philippians 4:7-9 says, *"And the peace of God, which passeth all understanding, shall keep your hearts and minds through Christ Jesus. Finally, brethren, whatsoever things are true, whatsoever things are honest, whatsoever things are just, whatsoever things are pure, whatsoever things are lovely, whatsoever things are of a good report; if there be any virtue, and if there be any praise, think on these things. Those things, which ye have learned, and received, and heard, and seen in me, do: and the God of peace will be with you."*

Peace protects the heart and the mind. If our peace does not pass our understanding, we need more peace. Another thought is this. We do not have to understand a storm to have peace in it. As Jesus slept in the storm, his peace passed the disciples understanding. *When our affections are set on the things above, our circumstances do not cause us to lose our peace.*

Paul said to the Colossians, *"set your affections on the things above."* This means to think on or exercise your mind on the things above. This is one of the ways we fulfill the great commandment of loving God with all of our heart, soul, mind and strength. Paul explains in Philippians how to set your affections on the things above, when he says, *"think on these things."* This is one of the keys to keeping a renewed mind and creating an environment in your mind that can hear the still small voice of the Holy Spirit. Hearing his voice will also allow us to see the will of God clearly. Our mind determines what we hear and see in the natural, and so it is in the Spirit. That is why we have been given the mind of Christ. Our mind converts what we hear and see.

The new heart we are given in the new covenant is only compatible with the mind of Christ. The new heart and a carnal mind will not work well together; however, many Christians live very frustrated due to the fact that they may have a heart and head disconnect. I know first hand the pain of having a heart and head disconnect, but that is another story for another day. In the natural world, if my heart and head become disconnected my brain is no longer telling my heart to pump blood, and I will die, so it is in the Spirit. God's peace guards our heart and mind through Christ Jesus. If they are guided by the same attribute perhaps they should be connected. Jesus was tortured so we can have peace.

Jesus was beaten and crowned with thorns so that we could have the mind of Christ. The mind of Christ is to be protected by the helmet of salvation. Jesus was crowned with thorns so that we could be crowned with loving-kindness and tender mercies. When we are crowned with loving-kindness and tender mercies we can perceive and receive the thoughts that he thinks towards us through the mind of Christ. As we think about Jesus he gives us access to what he thinks about us. What is amazing about the mind of Christ is that it knows the heart of the Father.

> "For I know the thoughts I think toward you, saith the Lord, thoughts of peace, and not of evil, to give you an expected end."
> (Jeremiah 29:11)

Peace can guard our mind because he thinks thoughts of peace towards us. We will continue with the scripture passage above to see what knowing his thoughts towards us will produce.

> "Then shall ye call upon me, and ye shall go and pray unto me, and I will hearken unto you. And ye shall seek me, and find me, when ye shall search for me

> *with all your heart. And I will be found of you, saith the LORD: and I will turn away your captivity, and I will gather you from all the nations, and from all the places whither I have driven you, saith the LORD; and I will bring you again into the place whence I caused you to be carried away captive."* (Jeremiah 29:12-14)

His thoughts lead us to speak to him or call upon him; he then hearkens or draws near to us. We then seek him and find him and then he delivers us from captivity and the place we were bound in we begin to rule in instead. Training for reigning starts when his thoughts enter into our brain. When his thoughts enter into our brain, our mind is renewed and we receive the mind of Christ. We awake to righteousness as we hear his voice. We are conformed into his image from the inside out. We have his mind so let us think on him. Doctrinally we have the mind of Christ. Now we are walking it out experientially so that our doctrine and our life style are in agreement, that is what it looks like to walk in truth.

We can practice his presence and learn to hear his voice as we think on him. As we think on Jesus, it becomes very easy to hear him. Philippians says, 4:8 *"Finally, brethren, whatsoever things are true, whatsoever things are honest, whatsoever things are just, whatsoever things are pure, whatsoever things are lovely, whatsoever things are of a good report; if there be any virtue, and if there be any praise, think on these things."*

Thinking on Jesus

- Jesus is faithful and true, see Revelation 19:11
- He is the truth; therefore, he cannot lie so he is always honest, see John 14:6, Titus 1:2
- He is the Just one, and our Justification, see Isaiah 45:21, Romans 4:25
- He is the pure and spotless Lamb that was sacrificed for us, see 1 John 3:3, Proverbs 30:5
- He is all together lovely, see Song of Solomon 5:16, Psalm 27:4
- He is the gospel, see Mark 1:1, 2 Thessalonians 1:8
- Virtue was released from the hem of his garment, Mark 5:30
- He is worthy of praise, see 1 Peter 4:11

Spend 10 minutes meditating on who Jesus really is. Don't empty your mind; fill it with Jesus. Remember what he has done for you. See if you can remember three times when he broke into your life in a supernatural way and write them down.

Write down three times Jesus supernaturally intervened in your life:

1. _____
   _____

2. _____
   _____

3. _____
   _____

Chapter 10
A Godly Life and Spiritual Sight

The mind of Christ that we have been given, hears God when he is silent just like Jesus did in the Garden of Gethsemane. It also sees his will in the here and now and in the future. The mind of Christ allows us to see and hear spiritually. There are many people who can give you a prophetic word about your tomorrow but cannot clearly see what they should do today. This is the operation of a spiritual gift but the lack of spiritual virtue in the life of a believer. This person may be moving in the gift of prophecy but there is a true lack of intimacy when someone can tell you what to do and doesn't know what to do themselves. In the Bible, spiritual sight is directly linked to a godly life. Together, with the help of the precious Holy Spirit and the Holy Scriptures, we will see why many struggle with having clear direction in life. We will deal with this and conquer it together by the grace of God.

Psalm 34:8 says, *"O taste and see that the Lord is good: blessed is the man that trusteth in him."* Experiencing the goodness of the Lord opens our eyes to see spiritually. Sometimes we must experience something God does to see who he really is. Tasting God's goodness allows us to see spiritually the same way that his kindness leads us to repentance. We change the way we think about him after we taste his goodness and experience his kindness. The ultimate privilege of spiritual sight is to see the God who created and redeemed us. We were so created to see him; he created us in his very own image. There is a promise for the pure in heart and it directly involves Spiritual sight.

"Blessed are the pure in heart for they shall see God." (Matthew 5:8) Purity is necessary to see spiritually. If we do our part to stay pure, God will do his part to open our eyes to see him. The pure in heart did see God. Jesus was faithful to his Word even before he spoke it

into time and space. Here are some chapters that manifest this promise of the pure in heart seeing God. This promise was manifested even before it was made simply because Jesus is the same yesterday, today and forever. See these chapters to read about men who saw God: Isaiah 6, Ezekiel 1, Daniel 3,10, John 21 Acts 1, and 9 Revelation 1,4,5,19.

Many people have ears and do not hear; many people have eyes and do not see. This is a heart and lifestyle issue. Now most churches call Holiness legalism; however, we are commanded by God to be holy and separate. There is an amazing purpose behind it, and it is him! He tells us to be holy for he is Holy. He tells us to be like him so we can see him.

> *"Follow peace with all men, and holiness without which no man shall see the Lord."* (Hebrews 12:14)

Holiness in this verse means purity. *Purity gives us eyes to see.* The goal in seeing is to see the Lord because we become like what we behold. Jesus speaks to us and makes us clean by his word; we get to see him as we obey him and walk in purity. *Our choices greatly affect or infect our vision and purpose.* Jesus should be our vision and our purpose is to be conformed to his image and manifest his Kingdom here on planet earth. We can do this because we have the mind of Christ and we can hear him and see from his perspective. The mind of Christ can see what the Father is doing and partner with him through the Holy Spirit. Our eyes were not meant only to read, they were also meant to see in the Spirit. Reading the scriptures and living a pure life before the Lord should open our eyes to see who Jesus really is. Once we know him we can represent him properly. Jesus has been misrepresented by a lot of people who have ears and do not hear and eyes that do not see. The Father's desire is that we would hear Jesus. When our ears are opened, our eyes will be open to see the word of the Lord as Jeremiah mentioned. Jeremiah 2:31 says, *"O generation, see ye the word of the Lord. I have been a wilderness unto Israel? A land of darkness. Wherefore say my people, We are lords; we will come no more unto thee?"* The word of the Lord becomes visible to those who have ears to hear.

The Holy Spirit speaks what he hears and he also shows us things to come, so that we can position ourselves properly and accordingly.

> *"Howbeit when he, the Spirit of truth, is come, he will guide you into all truth: for he shall not speak of himself; but whatsoever he shall hear, that shall he speak: and he will show you things to come."* (John 16:13)

The mind of Christ can see what the Holy Spirit says. Both Jesus' and the Holy Spirit's success in ministry are based on their ability to speak what they hear, John 12:50. Perhaps it is very important that we can hear the Lord and see what he is saying to us. I am from God's favorite state, New Jersey the garden state. In New Jersey there is a commonly used phrase when someone is explaining something or telling a story, it is, *"Do you see what I am saying?"* I think that Jesus is asking us that? *"Do you see what I am saying, friend?"* That is just a thought. When we see what he is saying, we can partner with him in what he is doing.

God wants us to hear what he is saying so we can see what he has for us. There are also things God and the Holy Spirit want to show us so we can avoid unnecessary calamity, which comes through bad choices or a lack of wise choices. Usually someone who doesn't have wise counsel doesn't make wise choices. Someone who sees spiritually deeply understands their need for other people's perspectives on certain situations. The wisest man ever to live, only second to Jesus, said this in Proverbs 27:12, *"A prudent man forseeth the evil, and hideth himself; but the simple pass on and are punished."* Here prudence gives prophetic insight into the future, so we can avoid any unnecessary problems. The simple or the foolish person cannot see and ends up paying the price for their blindness. A prudent man avoids unnecessary evil or calamity and also knows where he is going.

"The wisdom of the prudent is to understand his way: but the folly of fools is deceit." (Proverbs 14:8) Here wisdom gives the prudent man spiritual sight to understand where he is going and what his purpose is along the way. Our journey is not just about our destination; it is the process of the journey that gets us ready for where we are going and what we are going to be entrusted with when we get there. *Deception is spiritual blindness to God given purpose.* Deception is not only false doctrine but it is also not going in the right direction. All backsliding is, is not moving forward. The prudent man not only sees what to hide from, but he sees through wisdom and understands where he is going. It is not just about where we are going; it is about who we are becoming in the process.

There is no quick fix to spiritual blindness. The process of discipline and correction is what deals with our issues until we have eyes to see. An issue that would cause spiritual blindness is unforgiveness or hatred.

"But he that hateth his brother is in darkness, and knoweth not whither he goeth, because that darkness hath blinded his eyes."
(1 John 2:11)

All anger or hatred does is veil our spiritual eyes. Remember our natural choices have spiritual consequences. Unforgiveness blinds our spiritual eyes. Many times people's unforgiveness for someone else stops them from going where God wants to take them. However, the Gospel of Jesus, which is forgiveness, opens our eyes if we would only believe.

"In whom the God of this world hath blinded the minds of them which believe not, lest the glorious gospel of Christ, who is the image of God, should shine unto them." (2 Corinthians 4:4)

Minds that are blinded do not have spiritual sight. Here this verse also shows us that if someone is spiritually blind it is the mind that is blinded. This truth bears further witness to the wisdom of God in creation.

The mind of Christ certainly is not blind; but it sees the will of the Father clearly. Blind eyes are also a symptom of a hard heart. John 12:40 says, *"He hath blinded their eyes, and hardened their heart; that they should not see with their eyes, nor understand with their heart, and be converted and I should heal them."* Many times we think that a lack of understanding is a head issue, but here it seems to be a heart issue. The writer of Hebrew says, *"by faith we understand."* Faith here seems to be a heart issue not a head issue. Sometimes we love God with all of our mind by simply turning our head off and believing with our heart what God has said or promised even when we cannot wrap our mind around it. The good news is we do not have to wrap our mind around it because we have been given his mind, the mind of Christ. There is a major connection between what God is saying and what we are seeing.

"The statues of the Lord are right, rejoicing the heart: the commandment of the Lord is pure, enlightening the eyes."
(Psalm 19:8)

What God says affects both our heart and our eyes. What is really interesting is what the word *enlightening* means in that verse. It literally means to *lighten* and set on fire. Our eyes are set on fire when the man whose eyes are like a flame of fire gives us a command, see Revelation 1:14. We do not just get his mind, but our eyes become like his when he speaks to us. God wants our hearts to burn and our eyes to burn as he speaks to us. (A side not is one time while I was obeying his commandment to cast out a demon in Haiti; the demon-possessed girl said, "There is fire in your eyes." The person did not want to look at me at all. When the demon left the girl she had no problem looking at me. I just wanted to share that random story with you.) When Jesus opened the scripture concerning himself to his disciples their hearts burned as he spoke. When he gave them the great commandment, their eyes were burning also, if Psalm 18:8 is true and it certainly is. God's word was like a fire in Jeremiah's bones, and it will be like a fire in this generation as well.

There are a people with eyes to see and ears to hear, and in my opinion that is you.

God wants us to have spiritual virtue so we can steward true prophetic insight properly. If we have favor without wisdom, we will not use the favor correctly. Divination is accurate information from an unclean source. We need accurate information from a pure source. The pure in heart see God. A prudent man can foresee evil and hide himself. Prophecy is what can be or what will absolutely be. One prophecy that *could have been* was Moses could have taken the people of God to the Promised Land, but he did not. A prophecy that will certainly come forth, no matter what, is *"Jesus will return and his feet will touch down on Mt. Zion."* (Revelation 14:1) The prudent understand where they are going through, wisdom. Wisdom is a spiritual virtue that gives direction. Direction and correction are needed for us to reach destiny. Our destiny is to be conformed into Jesus' image. We are conformed to his image as he speaks. When he speaks, he adds to us and his attributes are imparted. *What is free by impartation takes discipline to maintain and increase.* His attributes become our virtues, and they are what give us spiritual sight and insight. Sight is for the present and the future. Insight is for the past, as well present situations and circumstances. People with insight are very valuable in the Kingdom because they are navigators so to speak.

We are called to glory and virtue. As we spend time in the presence of the Lord, his virtue gets on us and we become like him. This same reality occurs when he speaks to us and shows us things. We become like Jesus as he interacts with us and we press into him. His realities become our experiences as we learn to really believe until we see. We do not have to see to believe; we have to believe until we see so that we grow into fully trusting. As I mentioned before, faith grows into trust as we go from sons who cry "Abba" to sons who cry, "Father." Someone who deeply trusts the Lord is someone who is spiritually mature. *A mature believer is a believer who sees, hears and obeys.* Spiritual maturity is seen and defined by spiritual purity. Our purity and authority are also directly linked. We are prepared to mature by subtracting some things, such as behaviors, habits and people from our lives. We mature as God adds his virtues to our lives. Peter said it really well;

> *"And beside this, giving all diligence, add to your faith virtue; and to virtue knowledge; And to knowledge temperance; and to patience godliness; And to patience godliness; And to godliness brotherly kindness; and to brotherly kindness charity. For if these things be in you, and abound, they make you that ye shall neither be barren nor unfruitful in the knowledge of our Lord Jesus Christ. But he that lacketh these things is blind, and cannot see afar off, and hath forgotten that he was purged from his old sins."* (2 Peter 2:5-9)

Jesus increases in us as we decrease to self. He loves and enjoys our unique personalities; however, he does not enjoy our self-life that becomes a conflict of interest between his Lordship and our choices. These verses are a great picture of the *"increase of his government"* in us. *Here we see clearly that a godly life produces spiritual sight.* Someone who is spiritually blind cannot see what is or what will be. The Laodiceans were blind to the fact that Jesus was not in their church. They could not see Jesus and they had an inaccurate understanding of their real spiritual condition. However, Jesus was not bashful; he confronted them and called them *blind, poor, naked, miserable and wretched*. He called them five names in perfect love, See Revelation 3:17-20. How is that for edifying! Spiritual blindness also causes people not to see into the future and prepare accordingly in the present. Someone who is spiritually blind is often looking into the past instead of the present and future. *Bondage has one direction and it is backwards.* We must press forward toward the high calling, which is in Christ Jesus. God expects us to be able to see where we are going, for his word is a l*amp unto our feet and a light unto our path.*

At first, Peter did not understand what the Lord said after his resurrection concerning his death. However, after he matured he was able to see. Jesus said to Peter feed my sheep.

> *"Verily, verily, I say unto thee, When thou wast young, thou girdest thyself, and walkest whiter thou wouldest: but when thou shalt be old, thou shalt stretch forth thy hands, and another shall gird thee, and carry thee whither thou wouldest not. This spake he, signifying by what death he should glorify God. And when he had spoken this, he said unto him, follow me."* (John 21:18-19)

Let us go back for a minute to where Peter is telling us to add different spiritual virtues to our lives. We will see that he says, if they abound, speaking of spiritual virtues we will not be barren or unfruitful in the knowledge of our Lord Jesus Christ. Yet those who lack those virtues are blind. Blindness and spiritual barrenness go together like rice and beans or like coffee and cream. Peter continues to say that we become spiritually blind when we forget that we have been forgiven. Forgetting that we have been forgiven often causes us to not forgive others when we are wronged. Hatred then begins to grow and, again according to 1 John 2:11, we become blind. As Peter continued his writing, just a few verses later, he told the people who he was writing to what was going to happen to him next. He could do that because through the grace of God he was empowered to live a godly life, which gave him spiritual sight.

> *"Knowing that shortly I must puff off this my tabernacle, even as our Lord Jesus Christ hath showed me."* (2 Peter 1:14)

People of destiny must have spiritual sight for their own lives. It is not enough to operate in the gift of prophecy and have vision for the lives of others. We must live a godly life and let God's word take root in our lives so we bear fruit for him as we see, hear, obey and follow him.

Questions

1. If prudence allows us to see evil before it unfolds, Biblically speaking are we responsible for warning others?

2. If doing what's right gives us spiritual sight over time does doing what's is wrong hinders us from seeing reality in a real and accurate way?

Prayer

Father let your attributes be my virtues. Holy Spirit would you give me the gift of discerning of spirits according to 1 Corinthians 12:10. Father thank you for the mind of Christ that gives me spiritual sight beyond today. Let your vision for my life be a blessing to my family, church, community and to the nations and even the generations to come. We ask this in the name of Jesus Christ.

Chapter 11
Hearing Discipline

Everyone wants to walk in his or her destiny. Even unsaved people want to live out their *full potential*. Our destinies and full potential is in Christ alone. He gives us a new heart and his mind to make this all possible. However, to walk in destiny there are several things that are necessary that must be done on our part. We will touch on two of them in this chapter but one in a more specific way. In order to walk in God's plans for our life, we must be able with the mind of Christ to think the thoughts that he thinks towards us. His thoughts towards us are the words that guide us. *Integrity* guides us in the natural and *Truth* guides us in the spiritual. Proverbs 11:3 says, *"The integrity of the upright shall guide them: but the perverseness of transgressors shall destroy them."* Integrity deals with our choices and truth deals with God's leading. John 16:13 states, *"Howbeit when he the Spirit of truth, is come, he shall guide you into all truth: for he shall not speak of himself; but whatsoever he shall hear, that shall he speak: and he will show you things to come."* The Spirit of Truth guides us into the depths of Jesus Christ, who is the truth. Again we see that the Holy Spirit speaks what he hears and shows us things to come. As God speaks and we hear, our eyes are opened to the things to come.

To maintain this walk, we need *diligence* to do what is right and discipline to get us back on the right track when we do what is wrong. Discipline can be used a few different ways. For example, discipline is spanking your child in love as the Proverbs of Solomon teach. Another form of discipline could be more positive and less painful. I will use my beautiful wife as an example. She is disciplined or self-controlled in her spending habits. We are equipped by God to be diligent and to receive discipline when necessary. *Someone who can receive discipline the right way is someone who is teachable.* Someone who is teachable is trustworthy and generally will be faithful to God and people.

> *"For God hath not given us a spirit of fear; but of power, and of love, and of a sound mind."* (2 Timothy 1:7)

A sound mind in this verse literally means a *"disciplined"* mind. A true disciple of the Lord Jesus has a sound mind, which is disciplined to be diligent and to move forward with perseverance. *Perseverance is patience in motion.* It is kind of like waiting on God and seeking after him while you are waiting for him. Diligence is discipline in forward motion. In the last chapter, 2 Peter 1:5 told us to, *"Give all diligence to add to your faith."* Certain virtues manifest spiritual sight so that we can see where we are and where we are going and be fruitful along the journey. To add to our faith we must diligently listen to the voice of God, which when it is heard becomes the word inside of us. As the word is heard, faith grows in us and Christ is formed in us. Everything else that is happening around us is assisting this process of growth and maturity in Christ. *Sometimes there has to be pressure on us and around us to do something in and with us.* Jesus is a wise master builder who knows all the building materials necessary to make us just like him.

God desired the Promised Land for Israel. The Father also has promises for the body of Christ corporately and also promises for us individually. These promises are great and precious; they make us partakers of the divine nature according to 1 Peter 1:4. According to Hebrews, it is through patience that we inherit the promises of God. In the Law, God gave Israel one thing they must do to receive what he had for them. This principle is still true today.

> *"And it shall come to pass, if thou shalt hearken diligently unto the voice of the Lord thy God, to observe and to do all his commandments which I commanded thee this day, that the Lord thy God will set thee on high above all nations of the earth: And all these blessings shall come on thee, and overtake the,*

if thou shalt hearken unto the voice of the Lord thy God." (Deuteronomy 28:1-2)

God's desire was for them to obey and be blessed. If we disobey we will be cursed, it is that simple. There is no gray area in God. A gray area means there is a shadow and in God there are no shadows, see James 1:17. One day the Holy Spirit whispered something to me I will never forget he said, "There is no gray area in outer darkness." Here he was illustrating to me the simplicity of the spiritual world. *Diligently listening is the key to faithfully obeying.* Where our affections are, our attention will be. We love what we pay consistent attention to. God's voice must be the focus of our lives, the way it was for Jesus. We have been set high above all the nations because we are seated with Christ in heavenly places. We are seated above so we can serve below. We are given access to heaven's resources to bring solutions to earth and point people to Jesus as the only source of temporary solutions and eternal salvation. As we do this, we are walking in destiny as we walk with the Lord, whose word is a lamp unto our feet and a light unto our path. There are certain things that keep us from destiny like sin and iniquity. Sin stops us from knowing God and iniquity stops him from knowing us.

"And then will I profess unto them, I never knew you: depart from me, ye that work iniquity." (Matthew 7:23)

The goal is to know God and have him know us. As we give ourselves to the one who gave himself for us, we become like him. When we really know him, it is seen in our behavior because light really does shine in the darkness. Light doesn't shine at the darkness; it shines in the darkness and the darkness does not overcome it.

If we do not and will not receive correction, we will be headed straight for deception. If we do not receive discipline, we will live with a lawless spirit and the fruit of that is iniquity. The blood of Jesus has broken the power of iniquity, but we have to choose to leave it behind and move forward with God. Our participation is necessary in the process. God is opening the ears of his church and here is how and why.

> *"He openeth also their ear to discipline, and commandeth that they return from iniquity. If they obey and serve him, they shall spend their days in prosperity, and their years in pleasures."*
> (Job 36:10-11)

Discipline is necessary if we want to be blessed. God specifically opens people's ears to discipline so they are free from iniquity so they can be entrusted with prosperity and live in godly pleasure. Discipline is necessary if we are going to live a Kingdom life now. In the Kingdom, there is only abundance and prosperity. Suffering and blessing are a part of the kingdom. Obeying God will cause us to be both blessed with persecution and also prosperity. At the right hand of the King there are pleasures forevermore.

> *"Thou wilt show me the path of life: in thy presence is fullness of joy; at thy right hand there are pleasures for evermore."*
> (Psalm 16:11)

That is our portion if we are willing to hear discipline. We must serve God wholeheartedly even in adversity and we must turn from all iniquity.

David was a man who walked with God. His revelation of who Jesus was was completely unsurpassed in his day. He was a spiritual entrepreneur. He went deep in God, and God went deep in him. Anyone who wants to walk in destiny must walk through discipline.

> *"For whom the Lord loveth he chasteneth, and scourgeth every son whom he receiveth."* (Hebrews 12:6)

Bastards and orphans do not receive discipline or correction properly. They interpret discipline or correction as rejection, which is clearly deception. There are a lot of bastards in the pulpit today.

These men are unapproachable; they have set up a religious hierarchy to protect their own greed and lust. Not to worries God will bring discipline and judgment if discipline is not enough to bring change. Remember Jesus wants his church back. If we desire to have a friendship with God, it begins with discipleship. Discipleship is the process of discipline that God brings to our lives as we follow Jesus. This causes us to mature and makes us ready to steward the mysteries of Christ and the power of God. *Both wisdom and power are necessary for destiny.* According to Paul the apostle, Jesus is the wisdom and power of God. *Wisdom is necessary if power is going to be sustainable.* Sometimes wisdom is simply received as God speaks and other times we ask and God gives; however, wisdom also comes as we go through the discipline of the Lord.

God's discipline is different from man's discipline. A man spanks his child and says, "Go to your room." God whacks us on the butt and says, "Come here and let me love the hell out of you!" The same way, the fear of the Lord should cause us to run to the Lord and not from him. Adam and Eve ran from the Lord while David ran to him. Repentance is us running to the Lord. The difference between Adam and David was David understood discipline.

"Yea, though I walk through the valley of the shadow of death, I will fear no evil: for thou art with me; thy rod and thy staff they comfort me. Thou preparest a table before me in the presence of mine enemies: thou anointest my head with oil; my cup runneth over."
(Psalm 23:4-5)

David found comfort even in adversity, which is real peace. He did not fear because the Lord was with him. He found comfort in the rod and the staff of the Lord. *The rod was for correction and the staff was protection.* David in maturity found comfort in the uncomfortable. We have been given the comforter because God has predestined, in his eternal wisdom, to send us into uncomfortable situations. As we walk with God through certain circumstances, we can find comfort in the comforter alone. The Holy Spirit comes to convict and comfort all in the same breathe, it is just who he is. He brings discipline to us so that we can be conformed to the image of Jesus and receive all that the Father has for us. Notice David mentions the rod and the staff before favor and the anointing. Eating with your enemies is a picture of the favor of God. Before favor there is wisdom and wisdom comes by discipline. *We need wisdom to know how to use favor properly.* Favor is for us but not about us. Meaning, favor is to get Jesus and the gospel places where he is and it is not. Favor is not to get you or me on TV, although it might. Favor is to put Jesus on display. Before favor or anointing there must be discipline. *The wisdom that is produced by discipline makes favor sustainable. Both power and favor are sustainable through wisdom.* To attain our God given destiny, we will need integrity and truth to guide us. *We will need diligence and discipline to prepare and teach us.* We will also need wisdom to sustain all that God has given us by his grace. All this flows from his love that is towards us in Christ Jesus.

David made some amazing discoveries about God as he pursued him with all of his heart. David slept with Bathsheba and then sent her husband off to be killed on the front line of the battle he was supposed to be leading. Beloved, when leaders don't play their position other people suffer because of it. Nathan the prophet came to him and confronted him with a parable. The parable was the hidden wisdom of God. God's wisdom must be revealed. *Revelation opens the door to wisdom.* David was convicted and godly sorrow brought about repentance as the scriptures teach. He then wrote Psalm 51. *In the place of deep repentance, deep revelation comes forth.* When we open our hearts, confess and repent, God opens his heart, reveals himself and fills us with wisdom and truth so that we can overcome what we are repenting of. Jesus is both the wisdom of God and the truth. Apart from him there is no wisdom or truth. In this Psalm, God revealed to David's heart and what he desired.

"Behold, thou desirest truth in the inward parts: and in the hidden part thou shalt make me to know wisdom." (Psalm 51:6)

In a moment of time, David went from confessing his sin to knowing what God desired on the inside of us and what that would produce. Repentance opens the door of revelation. Discipline and correction also open the door of revelation. We will see that more clearly later in this chapter.

Our relationship with God is personal. There are things that God wants to say to us personally. His jealousy for us is what draws us to him. When a man is overly jealous for a woman she may want to run away. However, God's jealousy is Holy; it is not out of insecurity like human jealousy but it is out of perfect love. *Therefore, his jealousy has the ability to draw us if we are sensitive to his voice.* His voice is there to draw us to him. God will personally address anything or anyone that has too much influence in our life. Idolatry is anything that comes before Jesus. Some people's greatest idol is their Pastor; another person's idol could be money or even the Virgin Mary. Anything that gets in the way of him and us he will address. He will speak about it to us so we are not seduced away from him by putting other things or people before him.

In the Song of Solomon, there is a story that makes these truths visible.

> Song of Solomon 2:10-16 says, *"My beloved spake, and said unto me, Rise up, my love, my fair one, and come away. For, lo, the winter is past, the rain is over and gone; The flowers appear on the earth; the time of the singing of birds is come, and the voice of the turtle is heard in our land; The fig tree putteth forth her green figs, and the vines with the tender grape give a good smell. Arise, my love, my fair one, and come away. O my dove, that art in the clefts of the rock, in the secret places of the stairs, let me see thy countenance, let me hear thy voice; for sweet is thy voice, and thy countenance is comely. Take us the foxes, the little foxes that spoil the vines: for our vines have tender grapes. My beloved is mine, and I am*

his: he feedeth among the lilies."

Here the bridegroom, who is a picture of Jesus, speaks to his bride. He says come away with me. (This can be understood as an allegory, *not* as doctrine) He is leading her to intimacy and separation from everything and everyone else but him. His desire is toward her and so he is calling her to himself. He first speaks of who she is to him, and then he tells her the season she is in. Solomon repeats himself by telling her to come away with him. He begins to tell her his desire to hear her voice. After all this, he addresses the issue that could deeply affect their relationship.

"Take us the foxes, the little foxes, that spoil the vines: for our vines have tender grapes. My beloved is mine, and I am his: he feedeth among the lilies." (Song of Solomon 2:15-16)

There is fruit in their relationship or in their co-laboring endeavor and he must address what could spoil that valuable fruit and so he does. He warns that it is the little foxes that could spoil the vine. Let's break it down. He is warning her about the little issues that can cause big problems if not dealt with timely, properly and entirely. Even in life, if we do not deal with our issues, they will deal with us. This is love and intimacy in the form of discipline. We read earlier that the *"Father disciplines those who he loves and receives."* Well, so does the Son because he only does what he sees the Father do and that is what the Father does. In this place of intimate discipline, she receives a revelation of who he is to her and who she is to him. This revelation came in his presence from his voice when he confronted the very thing that was hindering their labor of love and could possibly spoil their future. If we don't allow God to deal with us today, tomorrow may not be all that pretty. Nowhere before this in the Song of Solomon does she say that, *"he is hers and she is his."* This revelation came from his speaking identity and correction to her. She matured in love and began to walk in revelation. After she realizes who he is, she realizes whose she is. Then the bride begins to recognize what the beloved is doing.

"My beloved is mine, and I am his: he feedeth among the lilies."
(Song of Solomon 2:16)

She now knows what he is doing because she knows him. When people do not know what to do or what God is doing, it is usually because they really do not know him deeply. When God's discipline comes on our life, we begin to know him and mature. When we mature in intimacy, we can see more clearly what God is doing in and with us. The Lord's Discipline comes to certain areas of our life when his Lordship is absent or not visible to the world around us. Maturity comes through discipline. Maturity is the purity of Christ being seen in us. So we must allow him to open our ears to discipline, so we can spend our days in pleasure and prosperity even when we are walking through great adversity. Adversity trains us for prosperity. The same way failures train us for success.

Thoughts to Remember

1. Often the things we avoid most are what God uses to makes us who we are really called to be.

2. Trying to avoid discipline or correction will seriously impair our spiritual vision and also the direction of where our life is supposed to be going.

3. One of God's most profound expressions of love is his correction; it may not feel like love but it is.

Prayer

Father I invite the love of your correction and the wisdom of your discipline into my life. I ask you to make me just like Jesus at all costs. Please open my ears to hear what I may not want to hear so you can make me the person you have called me to be. Holy Spirit be my comforter in this process. I ask this in Jesus' name.

Chapter 12
Hearing Hindrances

When we come to God with a preconceived notion of what he will say, we will not be able to hear what he is saying. Religion has filled people with preconceived notions. This explains why we can have people who are Christians for twenty-five years but honestly struggle to hear from a God who they truly do love. If it is the summer and my thermostat is set on sixty-eight degrees and I want it to get cooler, it won't until I adjust it. The thermostat set on a temperature with another desired temperature is a good picture of what a preconceived notion is. Often time's preconceived notions are formed by disappointments, frustrations and rejections. All of those cause unbelief to grow in a heart that was not guarded properly.

If we do not believe what Jesus has said, we will clearly have trouble hearing what he is saying. In this chapter, we will lay out some things that hinder people from hearing God's voice or his now word to them personally. Before a problem is solved, first it must be diagnosed and analyzed correctly. After that, a proper solution can be prescribed. This chapter will be scriptural, practical and very applicable to your life and even to the lives God has given you influence in. We are going on a journey into the heart of God. We will begin this journey by analyzing what has hindered us both individually and corporately from hearing God's voice.

A huge part of the reason people have a hard time hearing God's voice today is because of the leaders of yesterday. However, we are not throwing stones at them but bringing solutions for now. This problem can be traced back at the very least to the Protestant reformation. The Catholic Church was charging people for salvation, too bad that is unbiblical because Christians charge people for conferences. The Catholics had a better deal going! However, the blood of Jesus alone could buy salvation, hence the words of Paul the apostle, *"For ye were bought with a price."* So the Protestants split from the Catholics for some very good reasons. They named us Protestants, meaning our enemies named and defined us. (The concept of us being named by our enemies came from one of Kris Vallotton's sermons that was featured on iBethel.org in Redding California where Bill Johnson is the Senior Leader.) Unfortunately, we still live with the ramifications of that problem today. The Catholic Church kept the scriptures from the people. We, as Protestants, have not kept the scriptures from people; however, we have failed as a whole to teach people how to hear God's voice for themselves. On top of not teaching people to biblically hear God's voice, men have twisted the scriptures for personal gain and misused them to get people to buy into their "vision" as the "set leader". Also, this generation is very Biblically illiterate. There is a very small amount of Pastors and leaders who teach their people to properly interpret and study the scriptures. If we don't know the word, we don't have anything to discern the voice of God. The word through the Holy Spirit is the discerner, so this is another reason why most Christians will follow the stupidest leaders who make all kinds of un-biblical and even anti-biblical statements. Not hearing God's voice will lead to following the wrong leaders. This has devastated thousands of lives, and the way healing will come is by new marching orders from Jesus, the good Shepherd who gives his life for the sheep.

There are many different reasons that people have not been taught to hear God for themselves. One reason is because many leaders do not hear God for themselves; another reason is people really do not know how to effectively teach others to hear God's voice Biblically. Some other reasons may be a leader's fear or insecurity or job security. Meaning if people can hear God, do they need us to be their life support? *Believers who do not hear God for themselves are spiritually on life support.* For some in the body of Christ, hearing the voice of God is not in their theological grid. *Others love control and you cannot control a believer who lives by what God is saying, especially when you know that the truth makes people free.* Last but not least, and I would say this is the majority's case, it was not revealed to them because the god of this world blinded their minds just as Paul the Apostle said. They just did not know. Let us give most Pastors and leaders the benefit of the doubt and say they just simply did not know that the Father's number one priority is to hear his Son. See Matthew 17. The Father spoke audibly in the Gospels three times. His only directive was, *"hear ye him"* referring to the disciples hearing Jesus. That is huge because he knows everything and only says one thing! Perhaps it was the most important thing to the Father that we hear his Son? If we spend more time listening to a man speak about God than God speaking about himself, who is really our God? Many leaders need to repent and ask Jesus to forgive them for trying to be the mediator between God and man. There is only one mediator between God and man and that is the God man Christ Jesus.

Now that we have a brief understanding of where this problem came from, we will look to the scriptures for the solution. I also have some experience with this and I am going to share some things that will be beneficial for you. My desire in this chapter is to get to the very core of the heart issues that cause our ears to be deaf spiritually. I would like to start by mentioning what was written about in the previous few chapters. When we fail to take correction, we will not be able to receive impartation correctly. Correction often times is what gives us new wineskins in preparation for new wine. Most of what God imparts to our life comes by him speaking. He either speaks prophetically or through scripture, dreams and visions, and even audibly when he chooses to.

> *"Neglect not the gift that is in thee, which was given thee by prophecy, with the laying on of hands of the presbytery."*
> (1 Timothy 4:14)

When we do not take correction, there is a crack in our spiritual foundation, and we cannot take the weight of impartation. A person, who will not hear correction, probably will not have direction in their life.

Adam LiVecchi

> *"Meditate upon these things; give thy self wholly to them; that thy profiting may appear to all."* (1 Timothy 4:15)

Most people want something to give themselves wholly to but have not received that thing because they have not been willing to receive the necessary correction which will patch up their cracked foundation. Again I will repeat that a cracked foundation will not be able to hold the weight of impartation. Remember in Psalm 23, before David mentioned a table prepared for him in the presence of his enemies or the anointing of his head with oil, which is God imparting himself to David for service, he first met and found comfort in God's rod and staff. So before David was anointed and released into service, he was disciplined and prepared privately for what God had for him to do publicly.

Sometimes we come to a place in God where we can go no further in him unless we allow him to deal with the things that are hindering us from moving forward with him. We as maturing believers must give ourselves to this process. This painful process produces patience. In Luke 21:19, Jesus said, *"in your patience ye possesses your souls."* Meaning we have rule over our mind, will and emotions through patience. *Someone who does not have rule over his or her mind will and emotions will inherently struggle to hear God's voice.* People who operate mainly by their emotions are usually not led by the Spirit's voice but by the circumstances their soul is subject to in this life. This means that satan becomes their Lord even though they go to church every Sunday. When we do not know how to be silent and still and turn self off, it is hard to hear God. A picture of this in the natural would be of a person who doesn't have rule over his or her own spirit. This is someone who does not listen to others while having a conversation. This person is already thinking of what he or she is going to say back. I know because I used to be that person. Due to their mind being busy, they truly fail to listen and hear others. When someone has unconfessed sin they have an unclear conscience and their ability to focus intently is deeply impaired. *Also a double-minded person will have trouble hearing God's voice.* A natural picture of being double-minded would be trying to have two conversations at once. It becomes very hard to focus and hear. In the spirit realm that is what it looks like to be double minded.

> *"If any of you lack wisdom, let him ask of God, that giveth to all men liberally, and upbraideth not; and it shall be given him. But let him ask in faith, nothing wavering. For he that wavereth is like a wave of the sea driven with the wind and tossed. For let not that man think that he shall receive any thing of the Lord. A double minded man is unstable in all his ways."* (James 1:5-8)

We receive wisdom as God speaks; he imparts what we need through him speaking to us. If we are double minded we will deeply struggle to hear God or receive from him.

God changes who we are by speaking to us. John 15:3 says, *"Now ye are clean through the word which I have spoken unto you."* Purity is imparted as God speaks. Purity of heart happens as God speaks, which allows us to see spiritually. Remember Jesus said, *"The pure in heart shall see God."* So before God spoke to his disciples, they were obviously dirty or he would not have spoken and told them *"the word that I have spoken to you has made you clean."* He imparts identity, power and purpose to us so that we fulfill our destiny in him. To abide in him, his words must abide in us. Therefore, to truly abide in him, we must hear and obey him. *We leave the abiding place when we stop listening and obeying.* Another part of abiding is waiting on God. When we value someone, we are willing to listen to that person and spend time with him or her. A great majority of believers do not hear the Lord because they do not wait on him. Waiting with no distractions and with expectancy will help us to hear God. Silence is the key at times.

> *"But the LORD is in his holy temple: let all the earth keep silence before him."* (Habakkuk 2:20)

Perhaps God is calling for silence so he can speak? Sometimes reverence is spelled s-i-l-e-n-c-e. There are moments in God's presence where silence is the best option if we want to hear God. Moses was a man who knew how to wait on the Lord. In Exodus 24:16, Moses was in the manifested glory of the Lord on Mount Sinai for six days before God spoke one word to him. Sometimes just not waiting on God is a major hindrance to hearing him. Often we rattle off a list of prayers and say in "Jesus name" and get up without even giving God an opportunity to speak back to us. This is just plain rude. This kind of behavior is a sign of spiritual immaturity. Sadly to say that much of Christianity is not based on men and women hearing God, but what can be accomplished in the flesh. Do not worry, this will come to an end as God himself begins to shake everything that can be shaken as he has promised to in Haggai 2:6-7 says, *"For thus saith the LORD of hosts; Yet once, it is a little while, and I will shake the heavens, and the earth, and the sea, and the dry land; And I will shake all nations, and the desire of all nations shall come: and I will fill this house with glory, saith the LORD of hosts."* At the end of the shaking, the Word of the Lord will be left standing.

When we do not obey what God has revealed already, chances are he may not reveal more. Being faithful is one of the keys to consistently walking in revelation. Revelation comes as God speaks and as he opens our eyes to see the unseen realm of his Kingdom. Our ears will be deaf if we do not guard our hearts. *Our spiritual eyes will be blind if there are not spiritual virtues in our life as mentioned in 2 Peter 1:5-9.*

When people struggle to forgive, they will struggle with hearing God. The reason being is that we are forgiven because we forgive, and if we do not forgive, we are not forgiven. God speaks and we hear because we are forgiven.

"Now we know that God heareth not sinners: but if any man be a worshipper of God, and doeth his will, him he heareth."
(John 9:31)

If God does not hear sinners, they certainly do not hear him. However, he speaks to them; the problem is they do not hear his voice because they are not his sheep. So that is where you and I come in. God was speaking to heathen kings often in the Bible; yet the problem was that they did not hear his voice. So Joseph had to interpret Pharaoh's dream, and Daniel had to interpret Nebuchadnezzar's dream. They could interpret the dreams because they could hear God's voice. *Hearing God's voice is what makes us relevant to the world around us without compromising his Word.* A people who cannot hear God are useless to the world around them. The more we can hear God the more useful we are to partner with him.

Unconfessed sin causes shame. Shame causes people to run from God instead of to him. When Adam and Eve sinned, they ran from the Presence of the Lord. Running from the Lord and hearing from the Lord obviously do not fit. If we want to hear from him we need to run to him if we make a mistake and stay focused on him. Remember he is faithful and just to forgive us, *"If we confess our sins, he is faithful and just to forgive us our sins, and to cleanse us from all unrighteousness."* (1 John 1:9) He cleanses us by speaking to us, *"the word that I have spoken to you has made you clean."* A while back, I was sinning with my mind and mouth, and the Lord started speaking to immediately after that even before I could confess or repent. I asked him, "Jesus, what are you doing speaking to me? I was just sinning and now you are revealing something deep to me?" He answered and said, *"The word that I have spoken to you has made you clean."* When he said this, immediately, I began to weep as he was purifying my soul by his word. His word was washing over me like the sound of many waters. God's voice sounds like what he is doing at the time. His voice sounds like many waters when he is washing us from the uncleanness that sin brings.

Unresolved conflict creates confusion. Someone who struggles with confusion will not have clear direction for his or her life. Struggling with confusion will cause one to confuse God's voice with one's own thoughts. Confusion in the head is called being double-minded. Usually that person can recognize the devil's voice clearly but not God's. The reason being is because the enemy is the Author of Confusion and in that present moment he is writing their history, until the confusion gets broken and then peace comes back. When someone struggles with confusion, they will have a hard time making decisions. They will even get lost a lot when trying to find somewhere they have never already been. Confusion causes people to walk in circles because it stops them from hearing God's voice and direction for their life. When there is confusion in the leadership of a church, ministry or business they will take a step forward and two steps backwards. They will begin to gain momentum and then it will be stopped by confusion. Confusion often comes from a lack of identity. *People who do not know who they really are often struggle with what they are supposed to do and how they are supposed to do it.* When there is confusion, things that should be or are really clear seem obscure and unclear. A leader who operates in confusion will often appoint the wrong people into leadership positions. In the body of Christ, conflict is usually handled very poorly and so there is a lot of confusion that lingers often for even years at a time, which affects people's ability to hear God. Also the corporate atmosphere of the church is affected or should I say infected with confusion. A church with confusion doesn't discern how to move with the presence of the Lord.

Gossip, slander, coarse jesting and all forms of corrupt communication defile our ears and the ears of others around us. If you talk about someone's children repeatedly, how much do you think that person would want to speak to you? Gossiping is one of the things that makes hearing God nearly impossible, especially at a prayer meeting in the guise of, "I am really concerned about brother so and so." Sadly to say, I have been part of this evil behavior also. God forgive me. When people continually slander people, it is no wonder they are not going anywhere with God or in life. They cannot hear God clear enough to get to anywhere but church on Sunday. Gossip defiles those who speak and those who will listen to it.

> *"Looking diligently lest any man fail of the grace of God;*
> *lest any root of bitterness springing up trouble you,*
> *and thereby many be defiled."* (Hebrews 12:15)

One root of bitterness that springs out of one person's mouth will defile those who hear it. *Defiled ears will have a hard time hearing God.* This is why when there is conflict in a church many people do not hear God until the dust settles. Bitterness defiled people and they could not hear from God clearly. As a young man, I have already seen this happen several times. When ears are defiled, they will be hard of hearing until confession is made. Repentance comes and change occurs in the behavior. When we are slow to speak and quick to listen, hearing becomes easier.

> *"But now ye also put off these; anger; wrath; malice; blasphemy;*
> *filthy communication out of your mouth."* (Colossians 3:8)

When there is corrupt communication coming out of our mouths, it is hard to hear the proceeding word that is coming out of God's mouth. I personally know some of this stuff simply by making mistakes. I hope my transparency helps you to see any hindrances in your life. This chapter is not about any doctrine. I am not teaching doctrine; I am sharing experiences to help you see any possible road blocks in your walk with God.

A seared conscience makes it pretty hard to hear the voice of God. There are many things that sear a conscience. Continually resisting conviction and not taking correction will eventually sear a conscience. When a conscience is seared that person can no longer perceive things and situations as they really are. Their spiritual senses become dull because of perpetual sin. When a person has a seared conscience, they laugh at things that are really not funny. Sitting under false doctrine can sear your conscience also. *One of the things the scripture prescribes, as preventative medicine for a seared conscience is the confession of sin.* As we confess and repent, our consciences become clean and clear. This is what Paul said concerning conscience, as he was speaking to young Timothy about church leadership qualifications when he mentioned deacons.

> *"Holding the mystery of the faith in a pure conscience."*
> (1 Timothy 3:9)

A pure conscience is our wineskin for the mysteries of the Kingdom and the deep things of God that the Holy Spirit reveals. When our conscience is clear, we can hear from God and receive what he has for us. We can discern that it is God speaking and perceive what he wants us to do about what he is saying. When we hear the word in faith, most of the time we receive faith from the hearing. That faith shows us what we need to do next. Remember we walk by faith. Meaning that people who really believe God do something with what he has said if their senses are not too dull from a seared conscience.

A tender heart is a heart that hears and believes. A renewed mind is a mind that receives and perceives. A renewed mind and a tender heart stay possibly through a clear conscience. When someone's conscience is not clear they will have confusion. Confusion is the beginning stage of deception. Confusion messes up our perceptions, which makes it hard to hear from God. The importance of confessing sin is huge; it is part of what will keep your conscience clear. The keys to a clear conscience are trusting fully in Jesus' sacrifice, living righteously and confessing your sins when you are wrong. Also, it is necessary to forgive if we want to keep a clear conscience.

Despise not prophesying. When we despise prophecy, we are actually telling God we do not want to hear his voice. One of the ways we quench the Spirit of God is by despising prophecy or not wanting to hear prophecy.

> *"For the testimony of Jesus is the Spirit of Prophecy."*
> (Revelation 19:10b)

If we are not willing to hear God through someone else, why should he continue to speak to an arrogant person when he says in his word, "I resist the proud, but give grace to the humble"? One of the ways God resisted Israel was by not speaking to them for 400 years.

Sanctification is another key to hearing God's voice. Due to a lack of understanding, concerning sanctification many people struggle to hear the Lord. The more we sanctify ourselves, the easier it becomes to hear the voice of the Lord. Many people call sanctification legalism; however, that is people responding in the wrong spirit to a religious spirit or a controlling leader. In six or seven years of going to church, I have heard more about American Idol than I have heard about sanctification. Jesus himself said in John 17:19, *"And for their sakes I sanctify myself, that they might be sanctified by the truth."* If Jesus sanctified himself and he was God in the flesh who never sinned, how much more do we need to sanctify ourselves? All the generations who witnessed amazing revival and finished well were those who sanctified themselves and lived holy lives. Most of the revivalists that did not sanctify themselves did not finish well. We are sanctified by the *"logos"* word so we can hear and live by the *"rhema"* word.

"Sanctify them through thy truth: thy word is truth." (John 17:17)

The word in Greek used for *"word"* in this verse here is *"logos."* So through Jesus who is the truth we are sanctified. We are sanctified and set apart to hear from him and partner with him; this is the will of God. *His word in us connects his voice to us and we are led by the Spirit. The more we put his word on the inside of us, the easier it becomes to hear his voice.* He speaks often in context to what he has already said. There are probably many more hindrances that stop people from hearing God. A very simple one is disobedience. When we disobey, his voice becomes hard to hear, simply because sin hardens our heart. *A hardened heart will cause spiritual ears to be deaf and spiritual eyes to be blind.*

Bad theology causes people not to be able to hear the now word of God. God has been more misrepresented over the ages than any other person. There are so many misconceptions about who God really is, specifically in the person of his Son Jesus. There are so many false theologies and doctrines about who God is and what he does and does not do today that it has released a deaf and dumb spirit on the masses who have not been able to know God for themselves. When Jesus came the first time, the masses thought he was going to overthrow the Roman government and free Israel politically. However, he came to free them spiritually. Jesus came to die on the cross not to sit on Caesar's throne. The masses had a bad eschatology; it was like they never read Isaiah 53 or Psalm 22. Israel wanted Isaiah 63 before Isaiah 53 took place. Continuously he talked about the cross and his death but no one was listening, not even his disciples. This is why Moses and Elijah appeared at the mount of transfiguration. Luke 9:29-31 says, *"And as he prayed, the fashion of his countenance was altered, and his raiment was white and glistering. And, behold, there talked with him two men, which were Moses and Elias: Who appeared in glory, and spoke of his decease which he should accomplish at Jerusalem."*

It was almost as if due to their bad eschatology they could not hear God's voice or see what he was doing. Jesus was outside of their doctrine and outside of their theological box, but totally inside the scriptures because he was the Word. When he rode the colt into Jerusalem they screamed, *"Hosanna in the highest."* Israel thought that suddenly he would overthrow Rome and rule Jerusalem with an iron rod; however, they were wrong because that was not the season. That will take place at Jesus' second coming. So the multitudes went from singing *"Hosanna"* to screaming, *"Crucify him"* all because he did not do what they wanted according to their bad theology and bad eschatology. They were deceived and offended all because they did not have ears to hear what he was saying and so they did not know what he was doing. Offense really deafens ears and hardens hearts. We really need to guard our heart from disappointment. From disappointment, offense can grow if we do not guard our hearts. Offense will harden a heart and ruin a life, so let's look to Jesus to finish what he has begun in us. Let us get rid of all the hindrances that stop us from hearing his voice and obeying his word.

Questions

1. Can you think of any other hindrances when it comes to hearing God's voice?

2. Which hindrance in this chapter would you say is most relevant to your life?

3. Do you think being too busy affects your ability to develop ears to hear the voice of Jesus?

Prayer

Father, I ask you to take away everything that stops me from obeying you when you said to "hear your Son." My desire above all things is to hear and obey Jesus. Father would you give me grace to do what I need to do to partner with you in removing any hindrances from my life. I ask these things in Jesus' name.

Chapter 13
The Sword in His Mouth

Revelation 1:16 says, *"And he had in his right hand seven stars: and out of his mouth went a sharp two-edged sword: and his countenance was as the sun shineth in his strength."* Now that we know bad theology hinders us from hearing what God is saying, we are ready to see that good theology assists us to hear what God is saying. The tension of who Jesus fully is, releases the *mystery of Christ* that Paul mentioned in his epistles. He is fully God and fully man; oh the beauty of this mystery. He is a Lion and a Lamb; he is our Advocate and the Judge of the Nations. He does sit in the heavens and laugh, and he was even in a good mood in the Old Testament. He is in a good mood, and he will judge the living and the dead. He is the man of sorrows and for the joy set before him he did endure the cross through resurrection. According to Bill Johnson, senior Pastor of Bethel Church in Redding California, "Jesus Christ is perfect theology."

If you have seen Jesus you have seen the Father. However, not only the Jesus of the 4 Gospels but the Jesus of Daniel 10 and Revelation 1, the Jesus with a sword in his mouth, and the Jesus who is crowned with many crowns. Often when we think about Jesus, we forget that he eternally existed and was the Lamb slain from before the foundation of the world. Sometimes we forget that he is also the one who will judge the nations and rule with an iron rod from the city of David. Jesus will win the fight for Jerusalem. The sword of Islam is no match for the sword in Jesus' mouth. American imperialism and global government is no match for the Lord of Hosts. The reason why there is so much contention over that land is because it was promised to Israel. Jesus the King of kings, who is also the King of the Jews, shed his blood there making it the most valuable land on earth because the blood of God himself dripped off of Jesus' body onto that land while he hung on a tree. When we think of Jesus as a human, who he is and was, we tend to think of a gentle man with a beard, which he was. Often this is the Jesus people create religious concepts about. They try to box him into their unbelief or their one-hour nice little Sunday morning church service that is serving no one else but those that go. There is a Jesus with vengeance in his heart and fire in his eyes. This Jesus cannot fit into our little religious boxes. As a matter of fact, he will open his mouth and the sword that will come forth will cut that little religion's box to shreds. There is a generation who will not apologize for the Supremacy of Jesus Christ. Any generation that will successfully advance the Kingdom must preach the Supremacy of Christ. The Kingdom comes as Christ is preached.

If any chapter in this book has the ability to offend people, it is this one, so put on your seat belt and get ready for a side of Jesus that few people are willing to look at. Revelation must be progressive if we are going to move forward in the Kingdom. When Jesus revealed himself to Daniel, in Daniel chapter 10, Jesus had eyes that were like a flame of fire, but Daniel did not see a sword in Jesus' mouth as John the revelator did. When the Lord revealed himself to Isaiah, he revealed that there was a rod in his mouth, but John saw more detail he saw double-edged sword.

"But with righteousness shall he judge the poor, and reprove with equity for the meek of the earth: and he shall smite the earth with the rod of his mouth, and with the breath of his lips he shall slay the wicked." (Isaiah 11:4)

The wicked are slain by the goodness and kindness of God by the Gospel in the spiritual. Yet if the gospel is not received, eternal judgment from the mouth of God himself will be pronounced on them through torture and fire forever. I believe God wants to grip the church with this reality once again. People are really perishing, and so we must awaken out of this slumber and preach Jesus with fire, passion, love, truth and power.

We awake at the sound of his voice. Song of Solomon 5:2 says *"I sleep, but my heart waketh: it is the voice of my beloved that knocketh, saying, Open to me, my sister, my love, my dove, my undefiled: for my head is filled with dew, and my locks with the drops of the night."* The moral here is that it is his voice that tells us who we are and wakes us up. There are two things that wake us up. One thing that awakens us is Jesus speaking to us about who we are to him. The second thing that awakens us is the sharpness of his word to us. It is the sound of his voice and the sharpness of his word that will awaken our souls in this hour. I will share a brief story about a personal awakening. As a young man I was in a prayer meeting with some other young people late at night. There was a girl there who at the time I liked. As I was praying, I was praying loud with a little bit of a motive of her noticing my spirituality. The Lord Jesus whispered something to me that cut my heart very deeply. He said, *"Adam, you are an attention thriving whore, you are using a gift I gave you to draw someone to you."* I immediately replied Lord, "that is not a Biblical way to speak to me." He immediately said, *"Turn to the book of Ezekiel."* Suddenly I turned to Ezekiel, at the obedience to God's voice, and I saw what he was saying.

"Wherefore, O harlot, hear the word of the LORD."
(Ezekiel 16:35)

This wounded my heart and opened my eyes to how God can speak. I just began to repent and began to ask him to purify my motives and forgive my sin. When I told people in the meeting what the Lord had said to me, they said that was not the Lord. So I just kind of laughed because I knew it was him, and I knew that it was his kindness that brought godly sorrow to me, and it had worked repentance in me. At that moment I did not care what anybody said; I had heard God and it had moved me closer to him and that was all that mattered to me. God's word even when it is sharp is designed to cut us to the heart so that we change our mind. Sometimes we must be cut to heart so that we change our mind. Jesus Christ is the same yesterday, today and forever. What he did in the Gospels he does today, what he said in the Prophets he can and will say today.

He is God and there is no other.

There are things that God said all through the Bible that were highly offensive, yet he does not apologize for them. I find that rather interesting. Jesus has the most amazing personality ever. The more we hear his voice the more we get to know him. After we get to know him, we get to know him in an even deeper way by having access to know his personality. There are people who know of him. There are people that know what he does. There are people who think they know what he does not do. Then there are people who know him and are getting to know his personality. I hope that we are the people who are getting to know him and his wonderful personality. His personality is usually contrary to the circumstances. When his disciples are worried, he is peaceful. Jesus has an amazing sense of humor.

"He that sitteth in the heavens shall laugh: the Lord shall have them in derision." (Psalm 2:4)

The nations are raging in Psalm 2 and Jesus is laughing. I mean really there is no one like him. In times of great adversity, his personality comes out.

"Then shall he speak unto them in his wrath, and vex them in his sore displeasure." (Psalm 2:5)

He goes from laughing to speaking in wrath and bringing trouble upon his enemies suddenly. Then he begins to talk to himself. For a long time I thought that Psalm 2:8 was Jesus telling us what to pray, now I am convinced it is actually the Father speaking to his Son after his glorious resurrection and ascension to the right hand of God.

"Ask of me, and I will give thee the heathen for thine inheritance, and the uttermost parts of the earth for thy possession."
(Psalm 2:8)

When God tells us to pray for something specific, it is because he really wants to give us what he is telling us to ask for. Also if God allows us to hear something he is saying it is because he wants to change our perspective to his perspective.

I will share another thing that the Lord Jesus said to me one day. As I was spending time with Jesus he spoke this to me, *"Maybe if you take the log out of your eye you would be able to see me, Adam."* I knew this was the Lord Jesus because he was speaking in first person, and he was the one who said the verse below. He was speaking to me right out of what he has said, so that I would have the ability see him. God speaks so that we can see. This cut me to the heart and caused me to confess my "log syndrome disease," so he could heal it. First we must acknowledge what is wrong and then he can help make it right.

> *"And why beholdest thou the mote that is in thy brother's eye, but considerest not the beam that is in thine own eye? Or how wilt thou say to thy brother, Let me pull out the mote out of thine eye; and, behold, a beam is in thine own eye? Thou hypocrite, first cast out the beam out of thine own eye; and then shalt thou see clearly to cast out the mote out of thy brother's eye."* (Matthew 7: 3-5)

Hypocrisy also causes spiritual blindness. Much of the church that is always discerning things about everyone else is actually blind to their own condition. Instead of crying out to God about the spiritual bareness in their church, city or region, they will focus on everyone else's problems. What is really interesting here is the dude that is focusing on other people's problems has a bigger problem. He is seeing their twig but he has a log, which seems almost like a miracle. I personally think we as a people need to just learn how to tremble at his Word and let Jesus build his church.

We are supposed to live by what God is saying even if what he is saying hurts. God told Lot and his family to *"not look back."* Lot's wife looked back and became a pillar of salt. Her disobedience cost her life. We live by what God is saying but the harsh reality is that most Christians do not want to tell you about it but people die by not listening to what God is saying. I have a friend who I pay to be my friend, just joking, just wrote that to see if you were paying attention. Anyway, I have a friend who was a youth Pastor in the inner city of Orange, New Jersey. There was a young man in his youth group who he warned. He warned a young man in his youth group that the friends he was with would cost him his life if he did not stop hanging out with them. The 16-year-old boy did not listen and six months later he was found with about eight bullets in his chest and he died. When God speaks to us, we must take it seriously because sometimes other people's lives depend on it. However, the young boy's sinful life seared his conscience and he did not have ears to hear. It was to his own destruction. This truly breaks my heart and God's. The enemy stole a life just because someone did not have ears to hear what the Spirit was saying to him. However, my friend was faithful to deliver the word of the Lord and so there is no blood on his hands. He could deliver a word like this because he knew and discerned it was the Lord, even though it was a sharp, cutting and confrontational word. Sometimes the things the Lord says are just like the sword in his mouth. Ezekiel 3:18 says, *"When I say unto the wicked, Thou shalt surely die; and thou givest him not warning, nor speakest to warn the wicked from his wicked way, to save his life; the same wicked man shall die in his iniquity; but his blood will I require at thine hand."* Intercession is not just praying sometimes it includes speaking and action also. Prayer without action is not intercession; it's verbalized unbelief.

Jesus allows the sharpness of his word to cut our hearts open so the brightness of his face can shine into and through our lives. His word is like the sword in his mouth; it is doubled edged. The sword is a sword of judgment and of mercy. Judgment is deserved and mercy is given if we receive Jesus. If not it is judgment alone. Sometimes people get mixed up between judgment and wrath.

Wrath is what Jesus bore in his body on the tree. *Wrath is the complete absence of God's mercy.* While even in God's judgments, he is merciful. In the Old Testament, God would judge Israel and have mercy on a remnant. The remnant that is alive would then know who God really is. In God's judgments, he releases the knowledge of who He is to those that survive.

Here are a few brief examples:

• Ezekiel 11:10 says, *"Ye shall fall by the sword; I will judge you in the border of Israel; and ye shall know that I am the LORD."*

• Ezekiel 25:17 states, *"And I will execute great vengeance upon them with furious rebukes; and they shall know that I am the LORD, when I shall lay my vengeance upon them."* That is the judgment side of the sword and here is the mercy side of the sword.

• Ezekiel 16:62 says, *"And I will establish my covenant with thee; and thou shalt know that I am the LORD."*

The sobering reality is the revelation of who Jesus is on both sides of the double-edged sword that is in his mouth. We are supposed to embrace all that Jesus is. The Jesus who loved the world enough to ransom his life for many is the same one who said, *"Narrow is the way, which leadeth unto life, and few there be that find it."* If you do not like that verse take that up with Jesus not me. His heart physically ruptured due to his body being stretched to the max on the cross. All of his blood poured out from his heart. He had a pierced side and wounded body. This same Jesus has a day of vengeance in his heart that no prayer meeting is going to stop. (See Isaiah 61:1-2 and Isaiah 63:1-4)

All that Jesus is and says will truly fascinate our hearts and minds if we have ears to hear and eyes to see. Sometimes the things God says are just plain unbelievable. What I mean by that is they are either really offensive or almost too good to be true; however, they are true. When Jesus calls Peter satan in Mark 8:33 that is a pretty strong word. Jesus never exaggerated or sinned at any time including that moment. The Father had to have been calling Peter satan because Jesus only said what he heard the Father say. That is bizarre to even think about. It's offensive to the mind and heart. However, Peter received a reality check from it. How about when God spoke to Joseph through a dream and said his whole family was going to bow before him. That was an amazing dream for the youngest son to have. He believed it and when he repeated it others were offended. Sometimes by simply believing the unbelievable and declaring it, others will be offended. I hope that this produces a fresh vision of how good God really is and also a fresh fear of the Lord that causes us to hear what he is really saying to us whether we want to hear it or not. If we are afraid to declare it, we probably won't live in it. We need the boldness to declare it and the courage to live the word out if we are really going to walk with Jesus.

Something that has been taught and said recently behind the pulpit is that, *"God is not judging people today."* That is totally false and unbiblical! The reality is his main thing is to save people, which is why Jesus came. However, God still releases judgments in the earth today. If God were not judging people today, Jesus would not be sitting at the Father's right hand ever living to make intercession for us. Some of the stuff I hear from *"charismania"* just makes me laugh or even want to cry; however, I still love *"charismania."* Jesus Christ is the same yesterday, today and forever according to the book of Hebrews. God is still in the business of healing, saving and judging people. "If" we are in an apostolic age, which we are, then the power of God is accessible to believing believers. Both Prophets and Apostles release the power of God. That power heals, saves and judges.

> *"For the time is come that judgment must begin at the house of God: and if it first begin at us, what shall the end be of them that obey not the gospel of God?"* (1 Peter 4:17)

Peter said judgment starts at the house of God; he did not say judgment is not for today. When prophetic people try to usurp scripture based on what they think or feel, they are wrong and need to humble themselves and repent. Judgment starting at the house of God was not a new concept for Peter. This truth is seen in the Old Testament and in the New Testament.

> *"Slay utterly old and young, both maids, and little children, and women: but come not near any man upon whom is the mark; and begin at my sanctuary. Then they began at the ancient men which were before the house."* (Ezekiel 9:6)

Also, in the book of Acts before the Angel of the Lord executed capital punishment on Herod after his speech, Ananias and Sapphira dropped dead at Peter's Word. They lied to God and left Peter's revival meeting in a body bag. Judgment started at the house of God and then it went to the civil government. This same thing happened in the book of Daniel. In Daniel 1:1 & Daniel 4:33, Jerusalem was besieged by Babylon and then the King was turned into a beast and ate grass for seven years. When the church is quick to prophesy judgment on the nation, watch out because it is coming to the church first. I do not get excited when God judges people or when people are turned over to their own foolish choices. I would always rather mercy; however, I echo the words of David with no apologies for Jesus or the two-edged sword in his mouth.

> *"The fear of the LORD is clean, enduring forever: the judgments of the LORD are true and righteous altogether. More to be desired are they than gold, yea, than much fine gold: sweeter also than honey and the honeycomb. Moreover by them is thy servant warned: and in keeping of them there is great reward."* (Psalm 19: 9-11)

Jesus releases correction so he can release blessing instead of judgment. He, in his goodness and patience, releases warning so we can turn from sin, so he does not have to release judgments. It is the pride of mankind that does not heed King Jesus' warnings.

Let us further examine the two-edged sword in the mouth of our Lord. The two-edged sword perhaps is a picture of the Spirit of Truth. The truth always confronts a lie or anything that binds the people of God because according to Jesus knowing the truth makes us free. Perhaps Jesus revealed the sword in his mouth to John the Revelator because of all the sharp things he was going to say to the seven churches in Asia? Jesus is talking to Pergamos.

> *"And to the angel of the church in Pergamos write; These things saith he which hath the sharp sword with two edges; I know thy works, and where thou dwellest, even where Satan's seat is: and thou holdest fast my name, and hast not denied my faith, even in those days wherein Antipas was my faithful martyr, who was slain among you, where Satan dwelleth. But I have a few things against thee, because thou hast there them that hold the doctrine of Balaam, who taught Balac to cast a stumbling block before the children of Israel, to eat things sacrificed unto idols, and to commit fornication. So hast thou also them that hold the doctrine of the Nicolaitans, which thing I hate. Repent or else I will come unto thee quickly, and will fight against them with the sword of my mouth. He that hath an ear, let him hear what the Spirit saith unto the churches; To him that overcometh will I give to eat of the hidden manna, and will give him a white stone, and in the stone a new name written, which no man knoweth saving he that receiveth it."* (Revelation 2:12-17)

This is actually a love letter from Jesus. It is written in red (in some Bible's) because he shed his blood for these people and he really loves them. However, he has some things against them, and he's not apologizing for his tone that is completely intolerant of sin.

Jesus prefaces what he said, by saying *"this is he with a two-edged sword in his mouth."* That is a pretty serious preface, isn't it? He has never ever begun a rebuke like this before. A word like this would cause anyone with a brain to tremble. The church is doing some good work but satan has a seat in the church. Then Jesus addresses two false doctrines; the first was the *"doctrine of Balaam."* This false teaching was producing sexual immorality and also idolatry. Sexual immorality is - idolatry of the flesh. Meaning self-gratification before obedience to God's word, which is idolatry without a statue. They were eating food sacrificed to idols. Then they had people in the church that practiced a false doctrine called the *"doctrine of the Nicolatians."* Jesus personally hated that doctrine. It seems like doctrine really matters to Jesus. When the church tolerates darkness, it is actually picking a fight with Jesus himself. Many people now a days say we do not split over doctrine. Well Jesus is about to split this church in half over doctrine with the two-edged sword in his mouth if they do not repent. Jesus, later in the book of Revelation, revealed that he would smite the nations with the Sword in his mouth. Before he does that, he is going to use his sword to fight against the people he died for because they are not living for him. Jesus does not say judgment is not for today. He says, *"Repent or I will come quickly, and will fight against them with the sword of my mouth."* I hope this creates sobriety in your mind and mine as the sharpness of Jesus' word cuts our hearts with conviction, so we can leave all compromise and man pleasing behind and follow Jesus. What am I saying? Well if you have ears to hear, here is what I am saying, **"Jesus wants his church back!"** Remember he's building a church and the gates of hell cannot prevail against it. If the gates of hell are prevailing against it then it's not his church and he obviously didn't build it. He paid for the church with his blood, and he really believes it is his. He does not think it belongs to bishop so and so. It is his and he wants it back!

I have found several of the most offensive Bible verses. I am going to list them below. Read them if you feel led, just joking. After them there will be a few verses about Jesus. I encourage you to take a Selah moment and meditate on Christ Jesus. Tell the devil to be

Adam LiVecchi

quiet; you are not too busy for Jesus. The verses are in no particular order. I pray that Jesus would be magnified as you mediate on him.

Meditating on Jesus

• **Romans 9:13** *"As it is written, Jacob have I loved, but Esau have I hated."* God, who is love, hated Esau? Esau sold something spiritual for something carnal.

• **Revelation 3:15-19** *"I know thy works, that thou art neither cold nor hot: I would thou wert cold or hot. So then because thou art lukewarm, and neither cold nor hot, I will spew thee out of my mouth. Because thou sayest, I am rich, and increased with goods, and have need of nothing; and knowest not that thou art wretched, and miserable, and poor, and blind, and naked: I counsel thee to buy of me gold tried in the fire, that thou mayest be rich; and white raiment, that thou mayest be clothed, and that the shame of thy nakedness do not appear; and anoint thine eyes with eye salve, that thou mayest see. As many as I love, I rebuke and chasten: be zealous therefore, and repent."* This is perfect love speaking. He calls them five names in perfect love. Really, there is no one like Jesus...

• **Revelation 2:22-23** *"Behold, I will cast her into a bed, and them that commit adultery with her into great tribulation, except they repent of their deeds. And I will kill her children with death; and all the churches shall know that I am he which searcheth the reins and hearts: and I will give unto every one of you according to your works."* Here Jesus is going to kill the children's church if the parents do not repent. This is radical; this is the side of Jesus we cannot fit into our religious boxes.

• **Revelation 19:19-21** *"And I saw the beast, and the kings of the earth, and their armies, gathered together to make war against him that sat on the horse, and against his army. And the beast was taken, and with him the false prophet that wrought miracles before him, with which he deceived them that had received the mark of the beast, and them that worshipped his image. These both were cast alive into a lake of fire burning with brimstone. And the remnant were slain with the sword of him that sat upon the horse, which sword proceeded out of his mouth: and all the fowls were filled with* *their flesh."* When the two-edged sword in his mouth cuts us deep in the heart, we will have ears to hear. Also his double-edged sword has a real way of getting rid of double mindedness. Let us think on Jesus together for a moment.

• **Revelation 19:10b – 16** *"For the testimony of Jesus is the spirit of prophecy. And I saw heaven opened, and behold a white horse; and he that sat upon him was called Faithful and True, and in righteousness he doth judge and make war. His eyes were as a flame of fire, and on his head were many crowns; and he had a name written, that no man knew, but he himself. And he was clothed with a vesture dipped in blood: and his name is called The Word of God. And the armies which were in heaven followed him upon white horses, clothed in fine linen, white and clean. And out of his mouth goeth a sharp sword, that with it he should smite the nations: and he shall rule them with a rod of iron: and he treadeth the winepress of the fierceness and wrath of Almighty God. And he hath on his vesture and on his thigh a name written, KING OF KINGS, AND LORD OF LORDS."* Here is a picture of Christ's supremacy. In this scene he is coming with vengeance to establish the fullness of his purchase on Calvary. When we see this Jesus, all variables are done and over with. He will rule on earth and nothing will stop him. This is a picture of the one our heart loves. Let us harden not our heart and hear his voice today and remember he is in a really good mood today.

Prayer

Jesus, let the sharpness of your word cut into the hardness of my heart. Lord let the brightness of your face shine on and through me as I hear and obey your word. Give me the boldness to say what you are saying and the courage to go where you are going. Father help me to love Jesus with all of my heart, mind, soul and strength. It's in Jesus name that I pray.

Chapter 14

Maturing in Our Ability to Hear the Voice of God

We know that God said some crazy stuff in the Bible, but what does that have to do with us today? Good question, I am glad you asked. We mature in our ability to hear God when he tells us stuff that sounds crazy to us. What do I mean by crazy? When I say crazy I am referring to stuff we really do not want to hear. In this chapter, I will do my best to make you see what I am saying. What is crazy to us is normal to God. Like the *"first shall be last and the last shall be first"* or *"you must humble yourself for God to exalt you when he is good and ready or in Bible terms in due season."* The benefits of hearing and doing what God tells us to do are very rewarding. If we hear God's voice and obey his word, our house will endure the storms of life. We need to build our house on the man who can sleep in storms. We must build our house on Jesus Christ the chief cornerstone. We actually become like him as we surrender our will. His will is that we surrender our will, which is how he makes us like him. This often happens when he tells us things we do not want to hear or tells us to do things that we do not want to do, or even tells us to go to places that we do not want to go to.

True intimacy with Jesus brings about transparency in our lives. Many leaders have been bitten by sheep and so they build walls to protect themselves. Almost anyone can build a wall, but it takes a skilled and courageous worker to build a bridge. That is why people who build bridges make like $120 an hour and people who build walls make like $25. (These are rough estimate wages in USD) If you build walls for a living as a construction worker that is honorable; I am sorry you got dragged into this illustration. The very thing hurt leaders build to protect themselves becomes their demise when they are no longer accountable to people or transparent about their life. In a short time I have seen this happen to people both first hand and also from a distance. We must guard our hearts and let the Lord be our shield. We are not our own protection. The moment we become our own protection we slowly enter into deception through trust in *"self."* The Angel of the Lord crippled Jacob and renamed him Israel or prince. From that day on he walked with a limp; so he would never put confidence in the flesh. *Everyone in the Kingdom walks with a limp.* What I mean is that most people have a profound weakness in their life and should be really sure to walk humbly and love mercy. We must be transparent and yet guard our hearts. An amazing picture of that would be a thermostat in a public high school. There is a clear hard plastic casing around the thermostat. It is transparent but locked, meaning it is visible and transparent but only the one with the key can open it. Jesus alone should have the key to our hearts, and his word should determine our climate. We can be transparent and yet guarded if we let him rule and reign in us as he speaks to us. That would be a very clear picture of spiritual maturity, while living transparently before men. We are in serious need of leaders who can let God mature them, and whose hearts are like the thermostat that only Jesus has access to. These are the men and women who will not faint in the day of adversity. Too many leaders make decisions based on the people instead of what God has said or is saying. Usually people who do that have a need to please people because of their own insecurities. We must allow the Lord to deal with us so we can make decisions based on his opinion alone.

Years ago, some of my friends and I would go to Life Center in Harrisburg, Pennsylvania. We would leave the conference so filled with Holy Spirit that we would minister on the streets afterwards. Really being filled with the Spirit will cause people to preach Jesus, not just keep them going to church night after night. One night we were on the streets of Harrisburg ministering prophetically. I was with a really good friend of mine named Brandon Vajda. I saw a young man in a white Cadillac Escalade. I was going to go preach Jesus to him, yet before I did I said, "Holy Spirit what are you doing?" He immediately answered, "I am resisting that man." That stunned me and messed up my theology. In a few moments, the Spirit of God reminded me that, *"God resists the proud, but gives grace to the humble."* That man was proud and God was resisting him. The Holy Spirit mentioned to me later, "I could talk to him in twenty years when he was on the street corner." What he was saying is when his sinful choices take him from the high life to rock bottom he will then be opened to the Jesus he really needs. The problem was his pride was blinding him to his desperate need for Jesus. I know that because I was once there before in my own life.

"The pride of thine heart hath deceived thee." (Obadiah 1:3 a)

Pride blinds. That is why we need people who will speak into our lives and make us accountable for our words, behavior and choices. It is very important to have people in our lives that tell us what we need to hear and not just what we want to hear. Controlling and insecure leaders who live with an identity crisis have "yes" men and woman around them who tell them mostly what they want to hear. However, wise leaders who know who they are and hear from God will have people around them who tell them things they do not want to hear. To keep David in check there was Nathan the prophet and Gad the seer around him, see 2 Samuel 24:11.

"And he set the Levites in the house of the LORD with cymbals, with psalteries, and with harps, according to the commandment of David, and of Gad the king's seer, and Nathan the prophet: for so was the commandment of the LORD by his prophets."
(2 Chronicles 29:25)

I cannot stress enough the importance of having Godly people around us who speak into our lives. It is a life or death matter. *For sustainable success and forward motion in life and ministry accountability is a must.*

God confronted David personally and also by the people God put in his life. It was Nathan the Prophet who confronted David and revealed David's sins in the form of a parable. The parable about sheep was really about when David slept with Bathsheba and sent her husband off to be killed in a battle he was supposed to be fighting. Perhaps Psalm 51 would not have been written if Nathan, whose name means *"God's gift,"* had been silent. Sometimes our silence keeps others trapped in their sin. Sometimes God's greatest gift to us is something that we do not want to hear but desperately need to hear. How many people through the ages have prayed and repented to God directly from the words of David in Psalm 51? Well they might not have if Nathan did not confront David. David being confronted by Nathan also helped train his heart for God's dealing that would take place later on in his life. Men and women who really love God simply know how to humble themselves and repent no matter what position, title or office they hold. When David humbled himself and repented, he received great revelation about God's desires and priorities. A man or woman who cannot truly humble themselves and repent just may fall one day and never get up. Humility is something that trains our ears to hear and our hearts to receive.

> *"LORD, thou hast heard the desire of the humble: thou wilt prepare their heart, thou wilt cause thine ear to hear."*
> (Psalm 10:17)

Humility is one of the keys to having ears to hear. When God is not resisting us because of pride, he is continually pursuing us with his word and presence. Humility affects our ability to hear God directly and also through others. Someone who is humble can hear the word of the Lord and the testimony of the Lord.

> *"I will bless the LORD at all times: his praise shall continually be in my mouth. My soul shall make her boast in the LORD: the humble shall hear thereof, and be glad."* (Psalm 34:1-2)

They can discern and recognize it even when it comes in a package they do not like, even if it is by a locust eating, camel skin wearing, and unshaven voice in the wilderness. *We will either be a voice in the wilderness or an echo in the pew.* We must choose wisely for it will drastically affect our life and the lives of others.

Sitting at His Feet

Our decisions to hear God and obey drastically affect our eternity and also generations to come. David was a man who loved God's voice and presence. Hell on earth for David was to be without God's voice and presence. He was a man who truly desired God above all else. David swore to God that he would do something and the very thing he swore to do, God told him not to do, pretty interesting huh? I wonder if we have ever been a similar situation.

> *"LORD, remember David, and all his afflictions: How he swore unto the LORD, and vowed unto the mighty God of Jacob; Surely I will not come into the tabernacle of my house, nor go up into my bed; I will not give sleep to mine eyes, or slumber to mine eyelids, Until I find out a place for the LORD, an habitation for the mighty God of Jacob."* (Psalm 132:1-4)

David swears to God that he is going to do something God tells him he is not going to do. This is death to self to the fullest degree. When we are ready to die to self, we are then ready to be entrusted with the greatest things that God has for our lives. In David's obedience, his love for God is seen more than his swearing to do something good for God that God has planned for someone else to do. The deepest desire that David had was to build God a house but God wanted David to love him more than his own desire to build God a house. God valued David's obedience to his word more than his building plans. When God told David not to build him a house, he listened and obeyed. His ability to hear made him a very integral part of what God was going to do concerning the building of his house in the next generation. If we obey God today, we will be an integral part of the future in a good way.

> *"Then David the king stood up upon his feet, and said, Hear me, my brethren, and my people: As for me, I had in mine heart to build an house of rest for the ark of the covenant of the LORD, and for the footstool of our God, and had made ready for the building: But God said unto me, Thou shalt not build an*

> *house for my name, because thou hast been a man of war, and hast shed blood."* (1 Chronicles 28:2-3)

Obedience is the ultimate test of love and loyalty. This one "yes" that David said to God probably meant more to God than many of his victories in battle. He won the battle of self. When we win this battle, we can be entrusted with what God has for us, and our lives become the preparation for the next generation to move forward in the Kingdom. When David said "yes" to God and "no" to self, God in turn prophetically included him in the building process of the house he wanted to build anyway.

> *"Then David gave to Solomon his son the pattern of the porch, and of the houses thereof, and of the treasuries thereof, and of the upper chambers thereof, and of the inner parlours thereof, and of the place of the mercy seat, And the pattern of all that he had by the spirit, of the courts of the house of the LORD, and of all the chambers round about, of the treasuries of the house of God, and of the treasuries of the dedicated things: Also for the courses of the priests and the Levites, and for all the work of the service of the house of the LORD, and for all the vessels of service in the house of the LORD."* (1 Chronicles 28: 11-13)

The Spirit of God revealed to David the exact measurements of the house of the Lord. If you continue to read 1 Chronicles 28, the Holy Spirit gave David the exact measurements and weights of the gold and silver instruments in the temple that were to be used by the Priests. He even received how the Ark of the Covenant would be laid with gold. The details that God gave to David were a reflection of David's intimacy with God. David told God the details of his heart and life and God told David the details of his home to be on earth. *The exact measurements were given to David because his heart was calibrated to God's voice.* The way our heart is calibrated to hear God's voice is by being completely dead to self. Most people do not want to hear that, but Jesus and I really do not care. It is more about what we need to hear than what we want to hear. As we mature in God we will learn to want what we need. When we learn to want what we need, we then really have eyes to see things, circumstances, people and even ourselves from God's perspective.

After the temple was finished being built by Solomon, he dedicated it to the Lord. On the day of it is dedication; the glory of the Lord came.

> *"It came even to pass, as the trumpeters and singers were as one, to make one sound to be heard in praising and thanking the LORD; and when they lifted up their voice with the trumpets and cymbals and instruments of music, and praised the LORD, saying, For he is good; for his mercy endureth forever: that then the house was filled with a cloud, even the house of the LORD; So that the priests could not stand to minister by reason of the cloud: for the glory of the LORD had filled the house of God."* (2 Chronicles 5:11-13)

I think this is very interesting how God gave David the exact pattern of the temple and how the day it was dedicated God himself came and inhabited every bit of occupy able space. When the Holy Spirit was revealing the pattern to David, every bit of it needed to be made according to God's plan because God himself was going to come and occupy the space that was set apart for him. *We make room for God to encounter people as we hear his voice and obey him. When God gives us a vision for our life it is because he plans to show up in it.* God gave David the structure he himself would show up in. The prophetic movement must have a value for structure and substance and patterns and positioning. Our success is defined by our obedience not necessarily by the results.

Hundreds of years later, the glory of God would depart from that temple due to people not listening to God's voice and not obeying his word. *Listening to his voice is what empowers us to obey his commands.* The manifest presence of the Lord stays with those who hear and obey God. The reason the manifest presence of God is not in most churches today is because people are not willing to listen and obey God. When we deviate from what God is saying, we disconnect ourselves from what he is doing.

> *"Now the word of the LORD came unto Jonah the son of Amittai, saying, Arise, go to Nineveh, that great city, and cry against it; for their wickedness is come up before me. But Jonah rose up to flee unto Tarshish from the presence of the LORD, and went down to Joppa; and he found a ship going to Tarshish: so he paid the fare thereof, and went down into it, to go with them unto Tarshish from the presence of the LORD."* (Jonah 1:1-3)

God's word was to go to Tarshish. When Jonah ran from what God commanded, he ran from his presence. We must not separate God's presence from his commands. It is in the obedience to his commands where we live in his manifest presence and have access to his power and resources. When God commissioned Moses, Moses was not satisfied to just have his power. He said, *"If you do not go with me I am not going."* Moses did not just care about having God's power to be successful; he truly desired his presence to be with him as a demarcation separating Israel from every other nation. *God separates on the inside by his word discerning the thoughts and the intents of our heart and he separates on the outside by his manifest presence being with us.* When his presence is with us, what was impossible becomes possible, logical and probable if we will only hear his voice and obey him. Friendship with God and maturity in God are defined by being obedient and faithful to him. We can only achieve this through his grace that is towards us through Christ Jesus. To God, ministry results are clearly not a sign of success.

> *"Not everyone that saith unto me, Lord, Lord, shall enter into the kingdom of heaven; but he that doeth the will of my Father which is in heaven. Many will say to me in that day, Lord, Lord, have we not*

prophesied in thy name? and in thy name have cast out devils? and in thy name done many wonderful works? And then will I profess unto them, I never knew you: depart from me, ye that work iniquity." (Matthew 7:21-23)

Unfortunately, good results do not spell success. God's definition of success is not miracles, prophecy, mega churches, or the remnant church with 20 people in it that think the only reason people don't want to join them is because they are so pure. Success is only in complete obedience.

When Israel was unsuccessful because of their disobedience to God's voice, God raised up Ezekiel the prophet. Here is what God said to him when he commissioned him,

"And he said unto me, Son of man, stand upon thy feet, and I will speak unto thee. And the spirit entered into me when he spake unto me, and set me upon my feet, that I heard him that spake unto me. And he said unto me, Son of man, I send thee to the children of Israel, to a rebellious nation that hath rebelled against me: they and their fathers have transgressed against me, even unto this very day. For they are impudent children and stiffhearted. I do send thee unto them; and thou shalt say unto them, Thus saith the Lord GOD. And they, whether they will hear, or whether they will forbear, (for they are a rebellious house,) yet shall know that there hath been a prophet among them" (Ezekiel 2:1-7).

Again we see the Spirit is present when the word is spoken. God commissioned Ezekiel to talk to a people who would not even listen to him. That would be like God telling you to spend your whole life making a website that no one will ever visit. Ezekiel was faithful to God beyond his understanding. Here he loves God with his mind in the fact that he does not have to understand God to obey him. This is an amazing picture of Jesus really being Lord of someone's life. When we come to this kind of maturity, God can entrust us with our destiny and the destinies of cities and nations. When leaders in the body of Christ move in this kind of obedience, the Lord will give us the nations as an inheritance. When we can deny ourselves, God can give us what we need because he knows we will not take it for ourselves but that we will use it for his purposes.

As the glory of God is departing from the very temple that God used to fully inhabit, God also judges Israel. He speaks about it to Ezekiel.

> *"Also the word of the LORD came unto me, saying, Son of man, behold, I take away from thee the desire of thine eyes with a stroke: yet neither shalt thou mourn nor weep, neither shall thy tears run down. Forbear to cry, make no mourning for the dead, bind the tire of thine head upon thee, and put on thy shoes upon thy feet, and cover not thy lips, and eat not the bread of men. So I spake unto the people in the morning: and at even my wife died; and I did in the morning as I was commanded. And the people said unto me, Wilt thou not tell us what these things are to us, that thou doest so? Then I answered them,The word of the LORD came unto me, saying, Speak unto the house of Israel, Thus saith the Lord GOD; Behold, I will profane my sanctuary, the excellency of your strength, the desire of your eyes, and that which your soul pitieth; and your sons and your daughters whom ye have left shall fall by the sword. And ye shall do as I have done: ye shall not cover your lips, nor eat the bread of men. And your tires shall be upon your heads, and your shoes upon your feet: ye shall not mourn nor weep; but ye shall pine away for your iniquities, and mourn one toward another. Thus Ezekiel is unto you a sign: according to all that he hath done shall ye do: and when this cometh, ye shall know that I am the Lord GOD."* (Ezekiel 24:15-24)

This was real edifying, huh? God tells Ezekiel after all his faithfulness in ministry, I am going to give your wife a stroke; she is going to die and you cannot cry. That is really encouraging, isn't it? However, Ezekiel faithfully responds and continues to obey God, and he faithfully delivers the word to Israel. The word of the Lord was ruling Ezekiel, which means God's word was controlling how he felt. When God's presence defines who we are, his word can define how we feel. This means Jesus is really Lord of our life like he was Lord of Ezekiel's life. His circumstances did not define how he felt; his natural affections did not determine how he felt. God's word determined how he felt. Again, this is the kind maturity that can steward destiny properly. This is a man who can be trusted. I do not want God or the devil to kill my wife or yours. However, I believe God wants to take an end time bride into such a deep love affair with him that only he controls how we feel, what we do and where we go. He will conform us to his image as he speaks to us and deals with us. God deals with our issues so they do not deal with us. He speaks to us to make us like him, so the world can see Jesus when they meet you and me. That is simply what he is doing in the earth today. Jesus understands that people need him and so he speaks to us. The question is, do we love him? And what will we do with what he is saying?

Questions

1. Do you have the right people around you like David did? Do you have people who will tell you what you need to hear when you need to hear it?

2. Are you like Nathan or Gad was to David? Has God put you in someone's life to love them enough to tell them what they need to hear and not what they want to hear?

3. Are you like Jonah running from something God has said? If so yield to him and be a blessing to others in the process.

Prayer

Father, I ask you to bring godly people around me. Also open my eyes to people who are already around me who I can trust enough to keep me accountable. Give me humility to listen to you, boldness to repeat what you're saying and courage to obey you. Let the world see my integrity that grows through accountability so they will want to hear your truth from my mouth. I ask this in Jesus' name.

Chapter 15
God is Speaking

I speak this verse over you in Jesus' name. Matthew 13:16 says, *"But blessed are your eyes, for they see: and your ears, for they hear."* You are his sheep. I am not saying that you smell or that you bite or stick your nose where it does not belong, like sheep do. I am simply saying you are his sheep and you hear his voice and you are going to follow him wherever he will go. His voice empowers us to obey and follow. God knows everything, and he knows where he is going and exactly what he wants to do and when; therefore, he has a lot to say. The issue is not, "is God speaking?" The real issue is are we listening? There are so many things God said in His word. He said what he said because he meant it. God is very intentional about what he says and does because he knows what the exact results of his speaking and acting will be. From what he has said, we can learn to discern his voice. God is three people and one God. Some call it *"the trinity"* or the *"Godhead 3in1."* The depth of this mystery will fascinate our hearts for all of eternity. Jesus is seated at the Father's right hand and the Holy Spirit is here on earth in believers. So they are separate people but not a divided person, which means they are one. They are fully in agreement, which makes them one even though they are three. I will give you a scripture to show you exactly what I believe and am saying. 1 John 5:7 *"For there are three that bear record in heaven, the Father, the Word, and the Holy Ghost: and these three are one."* I hope that I did not confuse you; the devil is the author of confusion, and he is not writing this book. So just be at peace because the Lord Jesus is your peace and he has given you his Holy Spirit that you might be led into all truth.

When Isaiah was being commissioned, he heard God speaking to himself. This is beyond fascinating to the renewed mind. Isaiah 6:8 says, *"Also I heard the voice of the Lord, saying, Whom shall I send, and who* *will go for **us**? Then said I, Here am I; send me."* Here is something really profound. When God speaks to you, answer him. The same concept is seen in the process of creation.

> *"And God said, Let us make man in our image, after our likeness: and let them have dominion over the fish of the sea, and over the fowl of the air, and over the cattle, and over all the earth, and over every creeping thing that creepeth upon the earth."* (Genesis 1:26)

Before God the Father does something significant, he talks to himself and runs it by Jesus and the Holy Spirit. There is a good lesson here for the body of Christ. Before we make decisions and tell everyone "the Lord told me to" perhaps we should talk about it first, or maybe even pray about it? God wants to give us access to what he is saying to us and even what he is saying amongst himself, which is why we have the mind of Christ. *The mind of Christ can see what the Father is doing and hear what the Spirit is saying.* That is stunning! Jesus overwhelms me every time I stop to think about him. As we move into maturity, our ears can hear and our hearts can discern who in God is speaking to us. I hope to be able to help you discern the voice of the Father, the voice of the Son and the voice of the Holy Spirit from a Biblical and experiential standpoint. I will list several scriptures that establish what most of us already believe anyway. God in three persons speaks.

The Father Speaks

• **Matthew 3:16-17** *"And Jesus, when he was baptized, went up straightway out of the water: and, lo, the heavens were opened unto him, and he saw the Spirit of God descending like a dove, and lighting upon him: And lo a voice from heaven, saying, This is my beloved Son, in whom I am well pleased."* - The false doctrine of oneness gets put out of business clearly in these two verses. Heaven is having a family reunion as the Spirit comes upon Jesus and the Father speaks audibly from heaven. Here the Son is waiting, the Holy Spirit is coming and the Father is speaking.

- **Matthew 17:5** *"While he yet spake, behold, a bright cloud overshadowed them: and behold a voice out of the cloud, which said, This is my beloved Son, in whom I am well pleased; hear ye him."* – Here as the Father is speaking, his voice reveals who Jesus is to him and commands us to hear him. The Father desires that we hear Jesus based on who Jesus is to the Father. The Father is endorsing Jesus' words. So we know that Jesus obviously speaks if the Father is telling us to hear him.
- **John 12:28** *"Father, glorify thy name. Then came there a voice from heaven, saying, I have both glorified it, and will glorify it again."* - Jesus is speaking to the Father and a voice from heaven responds. This is very clear to see this is the Father speaking. The Father is revealing his nature and the nature of the testimony. What he has done concerning his name; he will do again simply because of who he is.
- **John 12:49-50** *"For I have not spoken of myself; but the Father which sent me, he gave me a commandment, what I should say, and what I should speak. And I know that his commandment is life everlasting: whatsoever I speak therefore, even as the Father said unto me, so I speak."* - So here we see a clear picture of Jesus speaking that which he hears the Father speak.

The Son Speaks

- **Hebrews 1:1-3** *"God, who at sundry times and in divers manners spake in time past unto the fathers by the prophets, Hath in these last days spoken unto us by his Son, whom he hath appointed heir of all things, by whom also he made the worlds; Who being the brightness of his glory, and the express image of his person, and upholding all things by the word of his power, when he had by himself purged our sins, sat down on the right hand of the Majesty on high;"* – Jesus is clearly speaking to us, meaning the body of Christ. Jesus is not just speaking to your Pastor or the Prophet; he is speaking to you, his beloved. He holds all things together with the word of his power. When we are not listing to him is when our lives begin to fall apart. He is speaking to the Father on our behalf and is speaking to us on the Father's behalf. There is one mediator between God and man and it is NOT the Virgin Mary. It is Jesus Christ the God man, fully God, fully man. When someone is partaking in idolatry they become like the idol they are worshipping deaf, dumb and blind.

• Jesus speaks all through the Gospels. He speaks in the book of Acts to Paul in chapter 9. He speaks to Peter in chapter 10 of Acts. He also speaks in the book of Revelation, in which He first reveals who he is, and then he speaks about the condition of the church. He then speaks of his judgments on the earth and then the new heaven and the new earth and everything under his leadership.

• **Revelation 2:7** *"He that hath an ear, let him hear what the Spirit saith unto the churches; To him that overcometh will I give to eat of the tree of life, which is in the midst of the paradise of God."* – Here we see an amazing similarity between the Father and the Son. The Father says to Jesus' disciples "hear him" speaking of Jesus. Then Jesus finishes his discourse to the church by saying he that hath ears to hear, let him hear what the Spirit "saith" to the church. Saith is the second tense of the word "said" meaning it is a continuum. It is not said or will say, it is a constant present tense. Meaning the Spirit of God is speaking to the church. What is amazing is that Jesus has just spoken very to the church, and he ends by saying hear what the Spirit "saith." The Sprit of God has an amazing job in regards to what Jesus has said and is saying. We will get into that in a moment.

The Holy Spirit Speaks

• Through the verse we just read it is very obvious that the Spirit of God is still speaking today. Here we will see how and what the Holy Spirit says.

• **John 15:26** *"But when the Comforter is come, whom I will send unto you from the Father, even the Spirit of truth, which proceedeth from the Father, he shall testify of me: And ye also shall bear witness, because ye have been with me from the beginning."* – The Spirit of truth speaks or testifies about Jesus. He is from the Father and sent by the Son. As we go deeper we will learn that the Father and the Spirit have a very deep and unique affection for Jesus.

- **John 16:13** *"Howbeit when he, the Spirit of truth, is come, he will guide you into all truth: for he shall not speak of himself; but whatsoever he shall hear, that shall he speak: and he will show you things to come"* – The Holy Spirit speaks what he hears. Both Jesus and the Holy Spirit's ministry are speaking what they hear. If we are going to have success in the Father's eyes we must learn to hear God speak.
- **1 Timothy 4:1** *"Now the Spirit speaketh expressly, that in the latter times some shall depart from the faith, giving heed to seducing spirits, and doctrines of devils;"* – In this verse "expressly" literally means distinctly. Here we learned that the Holy Spirit clearly articulates that which he says. There is clarity when he speaks. Jesus prophesied that the Holy Spirit would show you things to come. This prophecy came true and is coming true.

We have clearly established that one God in three persons speaks. We will begin by briefly speaking about the affection the Father and the Holy Spirit have for Jesus. As the Father and the Spirit speak to us, they release their love for Jesus. When this love gets in us, all fear goes from us, and we can follow Jesus wherever he will go.

"He saith unto them, But whom say ye that I am? And Simon Peter answered and said, Thou art the Christ, the Son of the living God. And Jesus answered and said unto him, Blessed art thou, Simon Bar–jona: for flesh and blood hath not revealed it unto thee, but my Father which is in heaven." (Matthew 16:15-17)

Jesus clearly shows us in this verse that the Father is the source of really knowing who Jesus is. It is the Father's hobby to reveal Jesus. It is the Father's good pleasure to give us the Kingdom as he reveals who the King is. The kingdom of God increases as the revelation of Jesus comes forth. The Father is nuts about Jesus; he is absolutely crazy about him. The Father is so proud of Jesus that is why his desire is to reveal him as we learn to hear him. The Father's favorite hobby is to reveal Jesus to us. So if God is speaking to you and revealing something new to you about who Jesus is there is a good chance the Father speaking. If Jesus is speaking to you it may be like this, "I am the resurrection and the life." The Father may say, "He is, or my Son the resurrection." The Holy Spirit may say, "Remember Jesus is the resurrection and the life."

What I am saying may sound different but it is actually very simple. We as humans are spirit, soul, and body. So if I am hungry my body is speaking to me. If I am feeling sad because of the circumstances in my life or I have just been disappointed my soul may be speaking. If I wake up at 3am speaking in tongues, it is probably my spirit speaking to me that I need to press in and speak God's language for a little while. These are all examples. *I am **not** making doctrines or any kind of authoritative statements;* I am only sharing thoughts and experiences that from my understanding are somewhat visible in scripture. *The Father reveals Jesus and the Spirit reminds us of what he has said.*

"But the Comforter, which is the Holy Ghost, whom the Father will send in my name, he shall teach you all things, and bring all things to your remembrance, whatsoever I have said unto you."
(John 14:26)

In this verse, the word remembrance means to put in mind. The Holy Spirit literally puts thoughts in our minds. Those thoughts are things that Jesus has said. In this verse, the Holy Spirit is teaching and reminding. It is the Spirit of God that properly applies the word of God. He knows the timing of God. The Holy Spirit is right on time. In Genesis 1 before Jesus ever spoke and said let there be light, he was hovering over the waters. The Holy Spirit was in position to perform the word as soon as Jesus spoke it. The Holy Spirit is the one who performs God's word. Jesus prophesied that the Holy Spirit would come in Acts 1 and the Holy Spirit in Acts 2 performed his word when he came.

The Father really has a passion for Jesus so much so that he had Jesus send the Spirit of truth, which proceeds from the Father. The Spirit of truth proceeds from the Father to testify of the Son.

It's like the Father and the Holy Spirit are talking about how much they love Jesus and, we are invited into that unspeakable joy and mystery.

"But when the Comforter is come, whom I will send unto you from the Father, even the Spirit of truth, which proceedeth from the Father, he shall testify of me." (John 15: 26)

Some of you reading may be like, what is your point? Well I really have no point. My only point is that the Father and the Holy Spirit are really and eternally passionate about revealing who Jesus is. This is so amazing it will even take place in heaven.

"And hath raised us up together, and made us sit together in heavenly places in Christ Jesus: That in the ages to come he might show the exceeding riches of his grace in his kindness toward us through Christ Jesus." (Ephesians 2:6-7)

Here the Apostle Paul is telling us where we are seated, which is in heavenly places in Christ. Then he prophesies about something that will happen in the present future and in the distant future. It will take God "ages" plural, which could mean thousands, hundreds of thousands or even possibly millions of years for him to reveal his Kindness that was given to us through Christ Jesus. The riches of his grace is his kindness. This is stunning, even in the age to come the Father will reveal his kindness toward us which came though Christ Jesus to us. Even in heaven it will take us a very long time to grasp just one of God's attributes in Christ. We will not be distracted by sin; we will see Jesus as he is. We will have new bodies and still it will take us ages just to comprehend one of God's attributes that are toward us through Christ Jesus. In timeless eternity, the Father will still be revealing to us the glory of his eternal Son.

Jesus loves the Father the way the Father loves the Son faithfully and eternally. We have been invited into the fellowship of this mystery. This is our inheritance as believers. Our family tree no longer matters; we have been grafted into the Tree of Life himself.

Jesus loved the Father's will so much he died for it. Therefore, Jesus loves to reveal the Father to us. It is his number one passion.

> *"All things are delivered unto me of my Father: and no man knoweth the Son, but the Father; neither knoweth any man the Father, save the Son, and he to whomsoever the Son will reveal him."* (Matthew 11:27)

The Son reveals who the Father is, but if the Father does not draw us to the Son we cannot come. No man comes to the Father but through the Son. This is so good it will fascinate us forever. We were created to know God. Having ears to hear is not just so that we will have something to say but also so that we will know God. When we really know God our life will say enough. Our words should be an explanation of what we are doing and not merely an explanation of what we believe.

I will briefly share some other things that Jesus likes to talk about. It is Jesus who told us that the Father waits and sees in secret. It is the Father who waits for his children in the secret place. The secret place is where the Father reveals who Jesus is. When the revelation of Jesus breaks forth in your life or mine that is the Father giving us what is most precious to him—Jesus. The Father has a house and the secret place is in his house.

> *"In my Father's house are many mansions: if it were not so, I would have told you. I go to prepare a place for you."* (John 14:2)

Jesus has made a place for you and I. It is the secret place and it is in the Father's house. Here Jesus is telling his disciples that there is room for them in the kingdom of God. Jesus loves to speak about the Kingdom. After he rose from the dead, he spoke to his disciples for forty days about the Kingdom of God.

> *"To whom also he showed himself alive after his passion by many infallible proofs, being seen of them forty days, and speaking of the things pertaining to the kingdom of God."* (Acts 1:3)

Here Jesus was revealing himself by undeniable manifestations or proofs, and his message was still the Kingdom of God. What is interesting is Jesus was not giving them a four spiritual laws manual. He was speaking to them about things concerning the Kingdom of God. Jesus loves the Kingdom of God. Another thing that Jesus loves to talk about is scripture. He is the word and so he likes to talk about scripture. In Daniel 10, a glorified Jesus with eyes like flames of fire makes reference to the scripture.

"But I will show thee that which is noted in the scripture of truth: and there is none that holdeth with me in these things, but Michael your prince." (Daniel 10:21)

In Luke 24, Jesus reveals himself in the scriptures while he walks about eight miles from Emmaus to Jerusalem with two of his disciples that did not know who he was, until he left.

"And beginning at Moses and all the prophets, he expounded unto them in all the scriptures the things concerning himself."
(Luke 24:27)

Jesus speaks about the scriptures when he was on earth, when he was glorified in his eternal state and also after his resurrection. Jesus will spend a good deal of the time speaking to you right from the scriptures. His name is the Word of God and he loves the word. Often times even when we are not reading the Bible at the moment Jesus will speak to us directly from it if we have ears to hear. The Holy Spirit will remind you of scriptures or help you apply them properly. Jesus will reveal them or correct you if you misapply them.

As we set our hearts to obey what God has said in his word, the Holy Spirit will speak to us concerning the times and seasons of our lives.

"And, behold, there was a man in Jerusalem, whose name was Simeon; and the same man was just and devout, waiting for the consolation of Israel: and the Holy Ghost was upon him. And it was

revealed unto him by the Holy Ghost, that he should not see death, before he had seen the Lord's Christ." (Luke 2:25-26)

Here the Holy Spirit is revealing that Simeon will see Jesus before he dies, which means Simeon was truly living by what God was saying. My Pastor David Greco told me that one. Here the Holy Spirit is speaking timing and destiny over Simeon and they both consummate in Christ Jesus. Jesus said, *"Go into all the world and preach to every creature"* and in the book of Acts the Holy Spirit gives very direct directives about what Jesus has already said.

"As they ministered to the Lord, and fasted, the Holy Ghost said, Separate me Barnabas and Saul for the work whereunto I have called them." (Acts 13:2)

Here the Holy Spirit is telling the church his delegation plan. The Holy Spirit is not asking he is telling. I have heard this phrase many times, "God is a gentleman." It makes me nauseous, God is God and he does what he pleases period. I know people who say that either really do not know him or are just repeating Christian lingo that has been beaten into them over the years. In the verse above the Holy Spirit is not asking for volunteers, he is actually commanding the church to do what he said and he is making it specific. If God is a gentleman, why did he knock Paul off his religious high horse? Why did he pick Ezekiel up by the hair? Why did he swallow Jonah into a whale? God is God and there is no other. Again he does what he pleases and that's final. He is Sovereign.

Later in the book of Acts, Paul wanted to go to Asia but the Holy Spirit stopped him. The reason being is that it was not God's plan for Paul at that time. God was actually sending him to Macedonia.

"Now when they had gone throughout Phrygia and the region of Galatia, and were forbidden of the Holy Ghost to preach the word in Asia." (Acts 16:6)

The Holy Spirit applies God's word to our lives properly and in the right timing. In Revelation 2 and 3, Jesus spoke loud and clear to the church. After he finished his discourse to each church, he would finish by saying, *"He that has ears to hear let him hear what the Spirit says to the church."* He said this because the Holy Spirit would come and remind them of what Jesus had just said and also bring personal application in the necessary timing. The Holy Spirit teaches, reminds, leads and guides. He was so happy to be in Jesus. Jesus never grieved him. Jesus is his favorite topic. The Father sent him in Jesus' name to remind us what Jesus has said and lead us in the way we should go at the time we should go there. Remember he is with you and will never leave you. Your ears do hear and your feet will follow.

Questions

1. Do you have an interest in discerning who of the Godhead is actually speaking to you?

2. Have you ever-heard God and knew it was the Father, Son or Holy Spirit specifically speaking to you? If so, write it down and thank him for this precious revelation.

Prayer

Father, let the Spirit of knowledge and understanding according to Isaiah 11:2 rest on me right now. Let me understand what I have just read. Remind me of what you have said and reveal to me if the Father, Son or Holy Spirit said it. I ask you to fill me with the knowledge of God and the mystery of his will with spiritual understanding. I pray this Father in Jesus' name.

Chapter 16
God Speaks Many Languages

We know that God does speak and is speaking. Hebrews 1:1-2 says, *"God, who at sundry times and in divers manners spake in time past unto the fathers by the prophets, Hath in these last days spoken unto us by his Son, whom he hath appointed heir of all things, by whom also he made the worlds."* We know that he speaks many different ways. Scripture shows us that he speaks through dreams, visions, the audible voice, and the still small voice of the Holy Spirit. He even spoke through Baalim the donkey. If the church does not speak, even the rocks will cry out. God speaks so many different ways and so many different languages. God speaks every dialect on this planet. He even speaks the tongues of angels. There is no one that God cannot communicate to. Everything he created he can communicate effectively to. The question is will we listen? I believe we will. I believe more than ever the people of God want to hear his voice. His voice is rooted in his word and out of his word he speaks. We must have a deep reverence for the scriptures. Christ must be supreme in our life. His word must be a priority in our life. *When his word is our priority, we will hear his voice.*

Many people can hear another language; the problem is few people understand what is being said. God wants us to know his languages. *The language of love is truth.* God is love and love always speaks the truth for they are inseparable. The Father is love, and Jesus is the truth. When the father opens up his mouth, Jesus comes forth. Love speaks the truth. One of God's love languages is truth. *Another one of God's languages is his commandments.* Jesus is the King of Kings. Kings give commands. His commands help us to see. Psalm 19:8 states, *"The statutes of the LORD are right, rejoicing the heart: the commandment of the LORD is pure, enlightening the eyes."*

Obeying the Lord's commands is the only prescription for success in the Kingdom. He tells us what to do, so as we obey, his will manifests in time and space. Obedience is crucial for our love for God to be visible to the world around us. Obedience is also crucial for our success in this life and in the age to come.

> *"Bless the LORD, ye his angels, that excel in strength, that do his commandments, hearkening unto the voice of his word."*
> (Psalm 103:20)

Here we see that angels hear the voice of his word, which are his commandments. He commands both the angels and us. Often times when there is a lack of the fear of the Lord, people struggle to hear the commandments of the Lord.

God speaks through miracles. Miracles train our heart to believe God and to change our minds to be able to see what he is doing. When I refer to miracles, I am referring to miracles that bring honor to Jesus.

> *"Because all those men which have seen my glory, and my miracles, which I did in Egypt and in the wilderness, and have tempted me now these ten times, and have not hearkened to my voice."*
> (Numbers 14:22)

The miracles were God speaking, but Israel did not have ears to hear. The generation that did not have ears to hear wandered, and they did not inherit what God had for them. Remember not hearing God is a very serious thing. God had promised them the Promised Land, but they did not get what he promised because they did not listen and obey what he commanded. What God is saying is what will get us where we are going. The love of God is unconditional; the promises and blessings of God are completely conditional. Eternal life is conditional, but God's love that sent Jesus was unconditional. God loved and so he gave, if we do not humble ourselves and confess and repent and believe, we will not be able to receive his greatest gift.

Another language that God speaks is the language of promise. The language of promise is amazing but it has blessing for obedience and cursing for disobedience. Many people really do not want to hear that but I really don't care. The truth is if we obey we will be blessed but if we do not obey, we will be cursed. There are many Christians who live under curses even though they do not have to because of the blood of Jesus. However, when our life does not agree with what the blood of Jesus speaks there is room for the curse to operate. I will give you a brief example. We as believers have the promise of healing because of the stripes on Jesus' back. This promise can be forfeited, read the following. Paul the Apostle is referencing communion.

> *"Wherefore whosoever shall eat this bread, and drink this cup of the Lord, unworthily, shall be guilty of the body and blood of the Lord. But let a man examine himself, and so let him eat of that bread, and drink of that cup. For he that eateth and drinketh unworthily, eateth and drinketh damnation to himself, not discerning the Lord's body. For this cause many are weak and sickly among you, and many sleep."*
> (1 Corinthians 11:27-30)

Taking communion before confession of sin and repentance can cause sickness or even premature death. Paul here literally describes the cause of these very problems in the Corinthian church. If someone were to say this today people would say, "Grace, grace do not judge, just love." In reality, we need to judge ourselves and align our behavior with the word of God. If we harden not our heart and obey God's word, we will live in all of the promises of God that are in Christ. We abide in Christ when we hear his voice and obey what he is saying. Promise and prophecy are very similar. There is some prophecy that I would categorize as sovereign prophecy, which will happen no matter what. Then there is conditional prophecy like, "if" you do this you will get that.

God speaks prophetically. Revelation 19:10 b states, *"worship God: for the testimony of Jesus is the spirit of prophecy."* Here we clearly see that the Spirit of Prophecy is the testimony of Jesus. *The centrality of all Holy Spirit outpouring is Christ Jesus.* When one of God's servants spoke to John the revelator, heaven opened and he saw a picture of Christ's Supremacy. *All prophecy is to magnify Christ.* It all comes from him and leads back to him; whether the prophecy is about his mercy or his judgments. The reality is he is an advocate and a judge and who he is must be revealed in the prophecy. Prophecy is the testimony of Jesus. True prophecy is what Jesus knows to be true. Our part is to step into the place of obedience in faith and partner with what he is saying. *Many times prophecy is an invitation to partnership.* God will say that he wants to do something or will do something and we respond and partner with him. This is an amazing privilege we have. Paul the apostle said that he wanted the Corinthians to learn to prophesy one by one. *When we learn, we are inevitably going to make mistakes, so have grace for people.* Take all prophecy to the scriptures and if it does not line up or if it is anti-scriptural just reject it. Pray and seek godly counsel about what you should do about a flaky prophecy. There are a lot of nutri-grain Christians involved in the prophetic movement. A nutri-grain Christian is someone who is nutty, fruity and flaky. Remember to be merciful and truthful and let the Holy Spirit lead you as you clean up a "soulish or fleshly" prophecy. Have I given one before? Yes, I have that's why I can boldly write about it with no shame. Please no one create a denomination called nutri-grain. If you do, this could be the slogan. "Nutri-grains where nuts, fruits and flakes can all agree to be wrong, unfiled, and completely led by the flesh. Membership is free. You don't even have to go to church as longs as you feel led not to go. It's ok." (This is a joke please don't take it seriously.) The sad part is that people get like that because authority figures have abused them, and that is not a joke.

God speaks the language of wisdom. Wisdom knows what to say and when. For example, if someone is really mad wisdom knows that a "soft answer turns away wrath." Wisdom knows to tell your children to look before they cross the street. *Wisdom warns people of danger and guides people into success.* Out of God's mouth comes wisdom. *Wisdom needs to get in us if we are going to be people who walk with the Lord and have success in that which he has called us to.* Through experience we gain wisdom. I will share with you something I learned by being wrong about something God told me. I heard God in a very clear way; however, I translated it the wrong way because I was still learning how he speaks. It was Sunday the 28th of November in 2005. As I was journaling, the Lord spoke to me and said, *"See what will happen on 11/20/2006."* He gave me the exact date of something that would transpire. I thought this was going to be something good, like meet my future wife or something. At that time I was single and single young men think meeting their wife will solve all of their problems. God was actually warning me to guard my heart on that day, but I did not know it. So in between November 2005 and November 2006, I went to Mexico and met a really nice and pretty girl. She ended up being my interpreter and so I was able to obtain her e-mail address and phone number. We emailed back and forth and then finally we spoke on the phone for the very first time on 11/20/2006, while I was visiting a friend in North Carolina named Ante'. I was sure that I had met my wife. However, I was wrong. God ahead of time was warning me but I thought it was him blessing me. He was blessing me with a warning so that I did not waste my time with something that was not from him. In my desire to hear God I heard him, but in my immaturity I did not interpret what he said properly. I am hoping that my failure to understand something God said to me will help you understand something God has said or will say to you. Mistakes and failures are the breeding grounds for accomplishments and success. *Remember learning and failing go together like persevering and succeeding.* It is ok to be wrong, yet it is not ok to stay wrong. If we want to maintain a posture of learning we must be teachable and willing to admit our mistakes. When we stop learning we become disqualified from teaching.

God speaks the language of mysteries. 1 Corinthians 14:1-2 says. *"Follow after charity, and desire spiritual gifts, but rather that ye may prophesy. For he that speaketh in an unknown tongue speaketh not unto men, but unto God: for no man understandeth him; howbeit in the spirit he speaketh mysteries."* If we are speaking directly to God he obviously speaks the language that we are speaking to him. God does not need a translator! Jesus spoke in parables, which is the language of mystery. Either God revealed it or people just did not get it. Many times Jesus did not even bother to explain himself.

"To understand a proverb, and the interpretation; the words of the wise, and their dark sayings." (Proverbs 1:6)

Many times in immaturity we hear God but do not really know how to respond. When we get wisdom and understanding we learn how to respond. Often times in dreams and visions, God is speaking in the language of mystery and it takes remembering what he said to hear what he is saying. When God reveals his mysteries to us we gain wisdom. The wisdom of God must be revealed not learned.

"But we speak the wisdom of God in a mystery, even the hidden wisdom, which God ordained before the world unto our glory." (1 Corinthians 2:7)

The wisdom that is hidden must be revealed or we cannot have it. Deuteronomy 29:29 says, *"The secret things belong unto the LORD our God: but those things which are revealed belong unto us and to our children forever, that we may do all the words of this law."* One of the ways God gives is by him revealing.

One of God's languages is giving. When he gives things or mercy, he is actually speaking. He gives bread to the hungry, a word to the weary, water to the thirsty, healing to the sick, and salvation to the perishing who accept him. God continually gives. He gives us dreams and visions. He has also given us the Holy Scriptures, which are the sixty-six books of the Bible. Jesus also gives material things. One day I was in need of money to pay a bill that was due very soon. I was getting ready to preach. Someone rang my doorbell and delivered me a nice Calvin Klein suit tailored to my size. This generous person had also given a fairly expensive watch to my wife as a gift. The total sum of these two gifts was no less than $ 800.00 USD. About a week prior I was asking the Lord for a black Calvin Klein suit even though I hardly wear suits. On top of that I already had a black suit. My wife also already had a black watch that I had bought her. The Lord Jesus spoke to me and said, *"I provided for what you didn't need to show you that I will certainly provide for what you do need, and I know where you live."* That really messed me up and I cried like a baby. However, the lesson I learned was priceless. When God blesses you with something you don't need when you have a need he is saying to you that he will meet the need. It's just who he is. He is Jehovah Jireh our provider. He gives us correction when we are wrong and blesses us when we are obedient. God really loves to give. Many people are seeking direction from the Lord. Jesus is our counselor and commander. Jesus, as our commander, gives commands that are not optional. However, when Jesus is counseling us he asks questions. He does not ask questions to learn, he asks questions to teach us. Jesus knew everything yet he asked questions. This is quite fascinating if we just stop to think about it. I encourage you to search the four Gospels and underline or write down all the questions that Jesus asked. Jesus asks us questions because the Father desires to reveal something to us. Wisdom asks questions so that revelation can come forth. Jesus doesn't ask questions because he doesn't know; he asks questions so we will learn.

Jesus, our counselor, cannot counsel us if we do not hear him. I am not against Christian counselors, but the need for so many of them simply is because people are not taught how to rightly divide the word of God and also because people are not taught to hear God's voice. *The body of Christ needs to be vaccinated of a religious hierarchy mentality.* Christianity is not about the supremacy of you, your Pastor or me; it is about the supremacy of Christ. Christ is supreme; therefore, we must desire to hear him and obey him above all things. When we listen to our Pastor more than God who is our God? I genuinely hope this book pushed you closer to Jesus, his voice and the Holy Scriptures. Christ's supremacy will be seen through our intimacy with him. When we hear and obey him, he becomes visible through us and his light shines for the world to see. That is the ministry the saints are being equipped for. That is what the Father is doing through the Holy Spirit in the church that Jesus is building. Let us tremble at his word and let him build his church. We are built up as he speaks. Remember you have ears to hear so keep listening.

Questions

1. Do you know any more of God's languages that you can see in scripture? This is a way you can connect with me via e-mail. If you find any that I have not mentioned please e-mail me at - info@we-seejesusministries.com

2. Do you spend more time weekly listening to God or your pastor? Who is your God?

3. What are you doing to develop you spiritual ears to hear God's voice? Do you think reading your Bible would make this process a lot smoother?

Study Suggestion

• Look through the four gospels and write down all the questions Jesus asked people, meditate on the scenes and ask the Holy Spirit to speak to you. This will be fun. You will learn about Jesus' personality.

• Look through the four gospels and write down all that Jesus commanded. Then categorize it by descriptive or prescriptive. When Peter walked on water that would be descriptive of something that happened. If you get out of a boat and try to walk on water you just may sink. When Jesus commanded his disciples to "go into all the world and preach the gospel to every creature" that was both descriptive for them and prescriptive for all of his followers everywhere in all generations.

Final Thoughts
The Urgency of His Voice

Developing ears to hear the voice of God is a must, especially if we are to live by every word that proceeds from God's mouth. *Our ears are developed as our minds are renewed by the washing of the word.*

"That he might sanctify and cleanse it with the washing of water by the word." (Ephesians 5:26)

Here Paul is speaking of the church. Jesus washes and sanctifies his church by his Word, which is why his voice sounds like many waters. Revelation 1:15 says, *"And his feet like unto fine brass, as if they burned in a furnace; and his voice as the sound of many waters."* God is so wise that his voice sounds like what he is doing with it. It sounds like many waters because his words washes and sanctifies.

Not only does God's voice sound like many waters that wash, his voice also is like the sound of a trumpet. A trumpet is to get our attention in an immediate way. A trumpet speaks of war, or an urgent call to attention.

"I was in the Spirit on the Lord's day, and heard behind me a great voice, as of a trumpet, Saying, I am Alpha and Omega, the first and the last: and, What thou seest, write in a book, and send it unto the seven churches which are in Asia; unto Ephesus, and unto Smyrna, and unto Pergamos, and unto Thyatira, and unto Sardis, and unto Philadelphia, and unto Laodicea. And I turned to see the voice that spake with me. And being turned, I saw seven golden candlesticks."
(Revelation 1:10-12)

In the Spirit you can see God's word. The sound of a trumpet causes John to turn right then and there. Our response to God must be immediate or we can actually miss the very moment he has created us for. The urgency of God's word to the churches was reflected in the initial way that John the revelator heard God's voice, *"as of a trumpet."* The lives of many other people were resting on the shoulders of one very old man. Remember God's government was on Jesus' shoulders, and we are his body. The government increases as the King speaks; therefore, we must learn to listen. To truly listen one must be quiet. John the revelator's ability to hear God was a life and death manner for seven churches in Asia Minor. Our ability to hear God is not only a life and death issue for us, but it is also a life and death issue for those around us. If Noah wouldn't have heard God's voice and obeyed, his whole family and all of the people on the earth would have been dead because of the flood. Beloved, remember God's word is a refuge for the obedient and a tidal wave for the disobedient. God's mercy was exhausted for those who would not hear Noah the preacher of righteousness and then the flood came. The people who chose not to listen chose death. We live in perilous times and must discern the urgency of God's voice. If Abraham hadn't heard God's voice, Isaac would have died. When we hear God's voice and obey, it really does affect other people. We must live by every word that proceeds out of God's mouth. Other people live because of our obedience or will perish because of our disobedience. Thank God Abraham had ears to hear. If Moses would not have heard God's voice three million people would have still been slaves for Pharaoh in Egypt. God's word is the truth, and it's the truth that sets people free. God's command to Moses was freedom for three million people. It's clear that what God is saying not only affects us but many other people as well.

The process of creation, redemption, reconciliation and judgment all are and were and always will be dependent on what God has said and is saying and will say. Therefore we must be dependent on that as well. Eternity itself is determined by what God has said, is saying and will say. Eternity depends on if we have ears to hear or not, remember the humble will hear.

> *"Then said he unto him, A certain man made a great supper, and bade many: And sent his servant at supper time to say to them that were bidden, Come; for all things are now ready. And they all with one consent began to make excuse. The first said unto him, I have bought a piece of ground, and I must needs go and see it: I pray thee have me excused. And another said, I have bought five yoke of oxen, and I go to prove them: I pray thee have me excused. And another said, I have married a wife, and therefore I cannot come."*(Luke 14:16-20)

This is a very sad story. Here there are three people who didn't have ears to hear. There came a "now" time and those who were invited didn't discern the invitation. There are times when God is very patient and then there are times where he expects an immediate response. The people didn't discern the hope of their calling or "invitation." But we must. My final words are, please take serious that which God speaks to you and just obey him. If you do you will see the realm of the miraculous activated in your life.

Notes

Notes

Notes

Notes

Notes

Adam LiVecchi, the leader of We See Jesus Minsitries, lives by faith and has a heart to bring the Word of the Lord to the Body of Christ. His ministry is an itinerant ministry based in Northern NJ. As a result of the Lord's leading he has had the opportunity to minister internationally in Hondorus, China, Mexico, Philippines, India, Peru, Dominican Republic, Brazil, Nicaragua, Haiti, Cuba, Canada, Uraguay, Uganda, Latvia, Estonia and all across the United States.

We See Jesus Ministries seeks to build the Kingdom of God through equipping the local church and delivering the Gospel message with signs and wonders follwing. Adam has the privilege of traveling with his beautiful wife, Sarah, and his brother, Aaron, who are both anointed musicians. Adam is also the co-leader of Voices in the Wilderness School of the Prophets with John Natale. Adam and Sarah LiVecchi look forward to building long lasting relationships that lead to sustainable change for the glory of King Jesus.

We See Jesus Ministries
31 Werneking Place
Little Ferry, NJ 07643
info@weseejesusministries.com
www.WeSeeJesusMinistries.com

Voices in the Wilderness
31 Werneking Place
Little Ferry, NJ 07643
info@voicesinthewilderness.us
www.VoicesintheWilderness.us

More Books by Adam LiVecchi

His Name is the Word of God
by Adam LiVecchi

Published by We See Jesus Ministries
Released 2010
Also available in Spanish

So You Want to Change the World?
Authors:
Don Nori Sr., Patricia King, Dee Collins, Rob Coscia, Barbie Breathitt, **Adam LiVecchi**, Abby H. Abildness, Dorsey Marshall, Doug Alexander, Lisa Jo Greer, Susan East, and Jim Wilbur

Published by Destiny Image
Released 2011

The Execution of Jesus Christ
by Adam LiVecchi

Published by We See Jesus Ministries
Released 2011

Available at
www.WeSeeJesusMinistries.com

Manuals by Adam LiVecchi

Go.Preach.Heal
A practical guide to supernatural living
Ministry Manual by Adam LiVecchi
Released 2011
Released in Portuguese & Spanish 2012

"As I read this latest work from Adam LiVecchi, once again I was challenged by his passion for Jesus. Over the past several years, I have had the opportunity to minister with Adam in a number of developing nations, both working side by side, and recently as he has gone to represent me. Adam's life and ministry are marked by his zeal to preach Christ everywhere he goes. This manual overviews those aspects of the faith that are central in Adam's life. Enjoy, and let Go.Preach.Heal provoke and inspire you."

Steve Stewart
Founder of Impact Nations
Author, When Everything Changes
www.ImpactNations.com

"Go.Preach.Heal: A Practical Guide to Supernatural Living has given us a simple but profound look at what the Christian life should look like. This book is filled with revelation that is beautifully partnered with practical advice on a wide range of everyday issues that helps the reader to live the way Jesus did. This is a wonderful book."

Bill Johnson
Author, When Heaven Invades Earth, and Essential Guide to Healing
Senior Pastor, Bethel Church, Redding, CA
www.iBethel.org

"Adam LiVecchi is a man on a mission to make Jesus famous to a generation that has largely strayed from a life of faith in Christ. The Go.Preach.Heal manual will introduce believers to a gospel of faith in action not mere words. I gladly recommend this manual for anyone wanting to mature in Christ and enter into the supernatural ministry Jesus has entrusted to the saints through the power of the Holy Spirit."

Adam Cates
Senior Pastor of the Big House Church
www.theBigHouseChurch.com

Listen.Learn.Obey
Prophetic Manual
Co-Authored by
John Natale & Adam LiVecchi
Released 2011

Voices in the Wilderness | School of the Prophets
www.VoicesintheWilderness.us

"There are many ministers in the body of Christ that call themselves prophets or prophetic people but haven't been trained in the word or in the sensitivity to hear God's voice. This manual will give those who hunger and thirst to develop an anointing and flow from the Holy Spirit that will mature them to use the prophetic gifts in the market place and in the church. This book is well needed in the body of Christ and I highly recommend it."

Prophet Jim Jorgensen
Sound the Trumpet Ministries International
www.SoundtheTrumpetMinistries.org

"If you hunger to walk in prophetic ministry Listen.Learn.Obey is for you. We have scores of books on prophetic ministry but this is a learners manual. This book puts practical tools in your hand. This book will not be an afternoon read but a seasonal soaking. You will work your way through this book and into a breakthrough. Adam LiVecchi is dedicated to God's own purpose of raising up a prophetic people."

Pastor Alan Hawkins
New Life City Church, Alberqurque, NM
www.NewLifeCity.org

"Adam and Sarah LiVecchi are personal friends of mine, I love them very much and I am honored to endorse Adam's newest book "Listen.Learn.Obey". In Matthew 16:18 Jesus said that the gates of hell would not prevail against the church. It's interesting to point out that gates are not mobile, they do not get up and attack, they are a fixed object. This is because the church is called to advance the Kingdom of Heaven and to live proactively instead of living reactively to the attacks of the enemy. Adam is a man of God who lives life proactively as he follows Jesus and this manual will equip and strengthen the body of Christ in the prophetic so that we can storm the gates of hell in all aspects of society. It's spiritual and practical, simple and yet profound. I highly endorse this manual especially for pastors and leaders who have a desire to be equipped and activated in the prophetic."

Nic Billman
Shores of Grace Ministries
www.ShoresofGrace.com

www.ingramcontent.com/pod-product-compliance
Lightning Source LLC
Chambersburg PA
CBHW072003290426
44109CB00018B/2115